THE WAY OF
KOREAN ZEN

THE WAY OF
KOREAN ZEN

by Kusan Sunim

translated by Martine Batchelor

*edited with an introduction
by* Stephen Batchelor

WEATHERHILL • *Boston & London* • 2009

Weatherhill
An imprint of Shambhala Publications, Inc.
Horticultural Hall
300 Massachusetts Avenue
Boston, Massachusetts 02115
www.shambhala.com

Printed in the United States of America

Distributed in the United States by Random House, Inc.,
and in Canada by Random House of Canada Ltd

Reproduced in Chapter Eight are Zen paintings by
Sokchong Sunim, a contemporary Korean Zen artist,
that were especially commissioned for this work.

The calligraphy on page ii, the characters for "one mind,"
is by Master Kusan.

The Library of Congress catalogues the previous edition
of this book as follows:
Kusan Sŏnsa.
The way of Korean Zen.
Translated from the Korean.
ISBN 978-0-8348-0201-8
ISBN 978-1-59030-686-4 (pbk.: alk. paper)
1. Zen Buddhism—Korea.
I. Batchelor, Stephen. II. Title.
BQ 9262.9.K7K87 1985 294.3'927'09519
84-25602

Deep in the valley of Mount Chogye
  a giant boulder shouts;
The lion's brain is shattered—the elephant
  has expired.
The vessel was huge and vast, his instruction
  steep and rigorous;
The teachings enveloped the world and
  his dignity stirred the oceans.

The mind-mirror is so limpid and bright;
Guest and host are both destroyed.
The brilliant shining is unobstructed;
All forms are vividly clear.

You opened your hand and space collapsed;
You clenched your fist and flowers bloomed on
  withered trees.
    Ha! Ha! Ha!
With the mind of a snake, the mouth of a Buddha,
  and the eyes of a ghost,
You majestically step into Avīci.

> —Songch'ol Sunim,
>   Patriarch of the Chogye Order,
>   on the occasion of Kusan Sunim's
>   death, December 1983.

Contents

Preface   *ix*

INTRODUCTION TO THE KOREAN
ZEN TRADITION, *by* Stephen Batchelor   *1*

1 A Short History of Buddhism in Korea   *3*
2 Songgwang Sa: Life in a Korean
  Zen Monastery   *34*
3 Master Kusan: A Biographical Sketch   *41*
4 Some Remarks on the Text   *52*

ESSENTIAL TEACHINGS OF THE STONE
  LION, *by* Kusan Sunim   *57*

5 Instructions for Meditation   *59*
6 Discourses From a Winter Retreat   *73*
7 Advice and Encouragement   *127*
8 The Ten Oxherding Pictures   *153*

Notes   *173*
Glossary   *176*

Preface

THE AIM of this book is to present the teachings of Zen Buddhism as they are traditionally taught in Korea today. To help place these teachings in their proper context, an introduction is included that tries to give a picture of their historical background and current monastic setting. The author, Ven. Kusan Sunim, was one of the most highly respected meditation masters of recent times in Korea.

During the last two years of his life, Master Kusan took an active interest in the preparation of this text. He willingly clarified many of the more difficult points in his teaching; provided us with relevant biographical material; and prepared several examples of his calligraphy to be used as illustrations for the book. He personally approved the first draft of the manuscript when it was presented to him at the end of 1982. The only substantial change made since then has been the inclusion of his commentary on the ten oxherding pictures, a tape recording of which was made available to us only after his death.

Since this book is intended for the general reader we have taken the liberty of omitting all the diacritical marks that, for scholarly accuracy, are usually found on certain Korean, Sanskrit, and Japanese words. Nevertheless, these marks have been retained in the glossary. We have followed the McCune-Reischauer system for transliterating Korean words into English. Chinese words are given in Pinyin romanization, with Wade-Giles equivalents given in the glossary. Since the Japanese word "Zen" is now part of the English language, we have used it throughout instead of the Korean "Son."

We would like to acknowledge the help of the following people in contributing to the completion of this work: Ven. Popchong Sunim, who clarified a number of technically difficult passages and traced many of the sources and references; Ven. Sokchong Sunim, who supplied the illustrations for the ten oxherding pictures; Ven. Wondu Sunim (Michael Roehm), who proofread the text and assisted in the initial stages of bringing the book to the public; Robert Buswell, who provided us with a typescript copy of the introduction to his book *The Korean Approach to Zen: The Collected Works of Chinul* and offered many valuable suggestions for the improvement of the original draft; and Henrik H. Sørensen, who initially suggested the idea of undertaking this project.

Martine (Fages) Batchelor
Stephen Batchelor

Songgwang Sa,
Korea, 1984

INTRODUCTION TO
THE KOREAN ZEN TRADITION

CHAPTER ONE

A Short History
of Buddhism in Korea

THE COUNTRY of Korea is formed of a peninsula of land jutting out into the East China Sea from the northeast coast of China below Manchuria. Its southeastern tip nearly connects to the arc of islands sweeping northwards known as Japan. Geographically it almost looks like a bridge between its two larger and more powerful neighbors. And throughout its history it has been frequently subjected to threats of invasion and domination by both China and Mongolia from the passes of the north and by Japan from across the sea. Armies from the feuding states in China have penetrated into its heartland and the Japanese have periodically tried to secure the country as a foothold on the Chinese mainland. More recently Korea has served as a battleground between Communist and non-Communist forces fighting to control the country.

Hence this small, rugged, and picturesque land, inhabited mainly by farmers and fishermen, has been and still is characterized as an area of disproportionate potential and actual political strife. This climate has given rise to a strong-willed and resilient people, one of whose principal drives is to create and sustain a sense of national unity and independence in the face of external pressures.

It is against this background that Buddhism was introduced into Korea over fifteen hundred years ago and has sustained itself as a living tradition up until the present day. To understand the successes and declines, the divisions and the reconciliations of the religion throughout its history in Korea, we must always bear in mind the political, social, and cultural atmosphere that has accompanied them.

Korea inherited its major cultural forms—Buddhism, Confucianism, and, to a lesser extent, Taoism—almost exclusively from China. Although it has evolved its own vernacular script, the traditional ecclesiastical and secular written form has largely been the Chinese ideogram. During the periods of its cultural formation it always remained within the Chinese sphere of influence. However, this was not solely a one-way process. In many instances native Korean scholars and priests were influential, through their writings and teachings, in China itself. The Koreans never allowed themselves to be the mere passive recipients of a superior culture: they invariably molded, adapted, and sought to improve upon the basic Chinese model. Nevertheless, although their religious and cultural traditions have developed a certain Korean character, they still bear the unmistakable stamp of Chinese origin.

Prior to the formal introduction of Buddhism, the religious practices of the Koreans consisted of animistic nature worship in which various gods, spirits, and other forces were invoked and honored, a belief in heaven and its influence through royal figures, as well as a primitive kind of ancestor worship. Many of these factors were never entirely replaced—at least among the common people—by the imported higher religions. Even nowadays shamanistic rituals are common in the countryside, and in many Buddhist temples will be found shrines devoted to the familiar figure of folk religion, the god of the mountain.

The distinctive phases of Buddhism in Korea correspond to the dynastic succession that characterizes and delineates the stages in Korean history. Five major periods can be distinguished: (1) the rule of the three kingdoms (Paekche, Koguryo, and Silla), 57–668; (2) the unified Silla dynasty, 668–935; (3) the Koryo dynasty, 935–1392; (4) the Yi dynasty, 1392–1910; and (5) the modern era, including the Japanese occupation from 1910–45 until the present-day state of partition into North and South Korea.

THE RULE OF THE THREE KINGDOMS
(A.D. 57–668)

During its early history before the final consolidation of the three kingdoms by the middle of the fourth century, Korea was the home of numerous tribal and nomadic groups originating mainly from different parts of Central Asia. Gradually, as the land became settled and various communities and power structures emerged, three separate kingdoms came into being. The first to be formed was Koguryo, which was situated in the northern half of the country including what are now parts of Manchuria. Next, the kingdom of Paekche arose in the southwest. And finally, Silla was established in the southeast of the peninsula.

Buddhism had already begun to find its way into China during the first century A.D. It was brought from India and Central Asia by merchants, scholars, monks, and travelers. When it first arrived it was given a mixed reception. Here and there small groups, often affiliated with native Taoist sects, began to show an interest in this strange, alien doctrine of India, but the majority of the people were content with the Confucian and Taoist philosophies of the then prosperous Han dynasty and felt little attraction toward Buddhism. Yet with the collapse of the Han dynasty in 220 and the loss of northern China to non-Chinese control, Buddhism started to increase in popularity in both parts of the divided country.

There are only scant records of the earliest encounters

with Buddhism in Korea. However, it is traditionally accepted that Buddhism was first introduced from northern China into the kingdom of Koguryo by the monk Sundo in 372. He brought with him images and scriptures and presented them to the king of that time, Sosurim. Shortly afterwards (384) an Indian or central Asian monk known as Malananda arrived in Paekche by ship from south China and was also received at the royal court. From these times onward it seems that Buddhism flourished in both kingdoms under royal patronage. It is also evident that the religion was adopted to a large extent by the rulers of Koguryo and Paekche in order to consolidate their newly won power by preaching the superiority and universality of Buddhism over the competing tribal faiths of the people. Moreover, the Buddhas, bodhisattvas and other figures in the Buddhist pantheon were promoted as deities of national protection, upon whose grace the prosperity and fortune of the realms depended.

Silla did not provide such a ready welcome for Buddhism. On its initial incursions it apparently met with much greater resistance from the aristocracy, who still adhered to the local religions. It was only officially accepted by King Pophung in 527 on the occasion of the martyrdom of his loyal minister Ich'adon. However, despite its tardy reception, Buddhism was most effectively incorporated into the society of Silla, playing a considerable role in the growing power of the kingdom as well as its eventual victory over the other two realms, which resulted in the political unification of the peninsula by 668.

One can find several examples of how the rulers of Silla employed Buddhism as a means of fulfilling their political ambitions. King Chinhung (540–75), the successor of King Pophung, himself received ordination as a monk toward the end of his life, thereby identifying secular with religious power. Such a sense of identity was also fostered by Chinhung and several of his successors by their taking the names of powerful figures from the Buddhist pantheon. It is during Chinhung's reign that the nationalistic youth movement call the *hwarang* was founded. This organization, which was designed to politically and militarily motivate the young men of the kingdom toward realizing the aims of the Silla rulers, was also associated with the Buddhist cult of Maitreya.

Such use of Buddhism for secular purposes likewise had its forerunners in China at this time. Emperor Wu of the Liang dynasty (r. 502–49) gave himself the title Emperor Bodhisattva and was an ardent Buddhist ruler. During the Northern Wei dynasty (386–534) the cult of Maitreya was highly popular and it was hoped that Maitreya would descend to earth in the Wei kingdom and from there start to unify the world. The emperor was likewise considered as an embodiment of the bodhisattva. In 589 China was finally united again under Emperor Wen (r. 581–604). To consolidate his power he made great efforts to unify his empire by means of Buddhism. This was the first time in which the religion was deliberately used as an instrument of state policy in China. His example exercised a considerable influence on his neighboring countries. All three of the Korean kingdoms sent envoys to Emperor Wen and returned home bearing some of the sacred relics which the Chinese ruler had enshrined in reliquaries throughout his country as a means of visibly unifying his realm.

In 660 Silla conquered the neighboring kingdom of Paekche and in 668, with the help of Tang-dynasty China, the northern kingdom of Koguryo, thus unifying the country for the first time. Because Buddhism had been developing for up to two hundred and fifty years throughout the peninsula, it now naturally became established as a unifying national religion. Since its introduction to Korea many monks had been sent to China and even India for training. They had returned with volumes of scripture, which they proceeded to translate and teach. Also during this time, in particular from Paekche, monks and envoys exported Buddhist statues and texts to Japan. They thereby helped prepare the way for the dissemination and development of the religion in Japan.

THE UNIFIED SILLA DYNASTY (668–935)

Having realized the political objective of unification, the ground was now prepared for the beginnings of one of the most productive and creative periods in the history of Korean Buddhism. Under the unified rule of the Silla dynasty the country now enjoyed relative political and economic stability free from the disruptive pressures of internal conflicts and disputes. Moreover, this period coincided with the Chinese Tang dynasty (618–907), during which Buddhist activity and influence reached their zenith in China. These two conditions, together with the work of several remarkable religious figures, allowed Buddhism to flourish to an unprecedented degree.

In order to establish a firm institutional foundation for the spread of Buddhism through the land, the government initiated the building of numerous monasteries and temples. Some of the most famous temples in Korea today—Haein Sa, Bulguk Sa, T'ongdo Sa, Pomo Sa, and Popchu Sa—were constructed during this period. The formal structure of monasticism, the rules and disciplines recorded in the Vinaya scriptures, had already been introduced into the country. In 526 the monk Kyomik returned from India to Paekche with many volumes of the Sanskrit Vinaya, which he then devoted the remainder of his life to translating into Chinese. In Silla itself the Vinaya had been imported from China by the monk Chajang in 643. Since Buddhism was held in such high esteem as the ideology and faith that had helped unite the country and was considered the sine qua non for further prosperity, numerous young men, including many of good education and high social position, were attracted to the monastic life.

Now that the religious community was growing and many facilities for study and devotion were being founded, the most important task became that of establishing the doctrinal and philosophical ideas of Buddhism in a coherent and solid manner. In China by this time numerous diverse schools of thought had grown up, each one centered around a particular scripture, group of scriptures or doctrinal trend introduced from India. The geographical vastness of China as well as the presence of different ethnic and dynastic groups easily permitted such a diversity of schools to emerge independently with little sectarian conflict. However, the narrower geographical confines of Korea as well as the need to preserve the unity of Buddhism for it to be able to serve as an effective social cement and national protector discouraged such a development. Hence, although several different doctrinal schools did emerge during the Silla dynasty, their divergence was compensated by a counter tendency to establish harmony between the various approaches. It is this syncretic emphasis that characterized the teachings of many of the greatest figures in Korean Buddhism and also came to be acknowledged as one of the distinctive features of Buddhism in Korea in general.

Five principal schools of Buddhist doctrine came into being in Korea during the first hundred years of the unified Silla dynasty. These were the Vinaya school, founded by Chajang; the Nirvana school of a monk called Podok; the Popsang, or Yogacara, school established by Chinp'yo; the Avatamsaka school; and the Popsong school. Of these five the most important in the future development of Korean Buddhism were the Avatamsaka and Popsong schools. The Avatamsaka (K. Hwaom) school was established by the monk Uisang (625–702). As with the founders of the Vinaya, Nirvana, and Yogacara schools, Uisang went to China to undertake his studies. In all he spent nine years there, returning to Korea in 670. The Avatamsaka Sutra is one of the most voluminous Mahayana texts, describing through various parables, narratives, images, and symbols a totalistic vision of the universe. Uisang studied under the second patriarch of the Chinese Avatamsaka school and was in close contact with Fazang (643–712), the best-known systemizer of the Avatamsaka philosophy.

The fifth doctrinal school, the Popsong (Dharma-nature) school, was founded by Wonhyo (617–86), one of the greatest and most original of all Buddhist thinkers produced in Korea. In contrast to the other schools, the Popsong was not centered around any particular scripture or traditional philosophy but was a syncretic approach that attempted to create a sense of unity among the various trends of thought present in Buddhism at that time. Furthermore, unlike the founders of the other schools, Wonhyo did not go to China to receive his training. Nevertheless, he was extensively read and the first Korean to produce a significant number of original writings. However, only about twenty of his works have survived to the present day. He was not concerned with merely preserving the doctrines of an imported sect from China but with creating an understanding of Buddhism that was relevant for his life and time in seventh-century Silla. For this reason, his school is sometimes called the Haedong (lit., "East of the Sea," i.e., Korea) school.

Wonhyo was born amidst the struggle for power between the three kingdoms and he died in the stability of a strong and unified nation. He lived at the time of transition when Buddhism ceased to be primarily an ideology used for unifying the people behind a certain leader and came to be recognized as a rich and complex religious tradition dedicated to wisdom and personal salvation. Not only his writings but also his life bore witness to his constant search for an integrated spiritual understanding. As a young monk he studied under numerous different teachers but apparently did not stay with any one of them for any length of time. At the age of thirty-four he left with his friend Uisang for China but abandoned this quest after coming to a sudden spiritual awakening while taking shelter one night in an old tomb. He returned to the turmoil of a warring kingdom and renounced the monkhood for a widowed princess who later bore him a son. Thereafter he referred to himself as just an "insignificant layman." He wandered through the country meditating and studying in the mountains and accepting shelter wherever it was offered him. He mingled freely among the people, instructing them in song and dance. He is reputed to have traveled around carrying a drum inscribed with the words: "Only one who is not disturbed by anything can immediately go beyond birth and death."

In his writings he strove both to reconcile the conflicting elements in Buddhist thought as well as to establish a single underlying doctrine that could serve as a positive basis for unifying apparent contradictions. His eclectic approach is presented in the remaining fragments of his *Reconciliation of Doctrinal Controversy Among the Ten Schools,* while his unifying philosophy is best expressed in his commentaries to Asvaghosa's *Awakening of Mahayana Faith.* His thinking centered around the notion of the one mind: while ignorant of this fundamental reality, sentient beings continuously suffer; but when enlightened to its inner nature and phenomenal activity, they gain peace and liberation. In addition to his attempt at creating a unified ideology to resolve scholastic disputes, he also propagated the doctrines of Pure Land Buddhism as a popular means of practice for the common people.

During the latter part of the Silla period an entirely different form of teaching, which was destined to play a predominant role in the future of Korean Buddhism, began to find its way into the kingdom. This was the tradition of Chan, pronounced Son in Korean, and popularly known nowadays by the Japanese term, Zen. To a large extent, the Zen movement arose as a reaction against the increasingly scholarly and abstract tendencies exhibited by the doctrinal schools in China. Moreover, it was the first approach to Buddhism that was uniquely Chinese in character. It expressed itself in terse, concrete images drawn from daily life and nature as opposed to the highly abstract, discursive and other-worldly Indian modes of expression. It emphasized direct experience through meditation rather than purely scholastic knowledge. According to tradition it was introduced into China from India by Bodhidharma in about 520. During the next four hundred years it grew steadily, attracted a large following, and eventually eclipsed most of the other Buddhist schools in the country.

Throughout the period of Zen's emergence in China the Koreans were in constant contact with many of the leading Chinese Buddhist figures of the time. Therefore, it would seem that they must have been aware of and to a certain extent influenced by the new movement of Zen. However, the doctrinal schools remained strong until well into the eighth century and the preliminary incursions of Zen teachers met with little enthusiasm. Nevertheless, as the scholastic traditions began to lose their vitality and became more institutionalized, and as the power of the Silla rulers began to wane and the kingdom started to fall into decline, people started to look for a new religious form which would provide them with a more dynamic and individual path of spiritual development.

According to tradition, Zen was first introduced into Silla by the Korean monk Pomnang at around 630. However, practically nothing is known of his activities or teaching except that he is reputed to have studied under the fourth patriarch of the Zen school in China. It is also maintained that his teaching was passed down through the monk Sinhaeng (d. 779) to Tohon (824–82), the founder of the first formal Zen school in Korea, the Mount Huiyang school. The actual origins of this first school, however, remain obscure.

In any case, the Zen tradition in China underwent its most important developments after the time of Pomnang. The era of Zen as it has been handed down to us today was ushered in by the sixth patriarch of the Chinese Chan school, Huineng (638–713). It was due to the efforts of such teachers as Huineng, his immediate disciple Shenhui (670–762), and his grand-disciple Mazu Daoyi (709–88) that Zen was given its characteristic style of expression and form. The first Korean to represent this more mature tradition of "sudden enlightenment" was Toui (d. 825). Toui left for China in 784 and became a disciple of Jizang (735–814), one of the most accomplished successors of Mazu. He remained in China for thirty-seven years before returning to Silla. When he eventually did come back in 821 he met with disinterest and a refusal on the part of the Koreans to listen to a teaching which seemed in complete contradiction with what they knew of Buddhism from the doctrinal schools. After unsuccessfully trying to propagate the Zen doctrine, he finally retired to Mount Sorak where he spent the remaining years of his life. In 862 his second-generation disciple Ch'ejung (803–80) founded the Mount Kaji school, naming Toui as its founder.

The response which Toui received to his teaching augured the future conflict which was to emerge and become ever more bitter between the doctrinal and Zen schools. The followers of the doctrinal traditions emphasized the necessity of studying the sutras passed down from the Buddha and gaining a clear intellectual understanding of the import of his teachings; the Zen teachers rejected such an approach as incapable of leading one to a real understanding of the true spirit of the Buddha's message. Instead, they emphasized the need to immediately break the mind free from the obscuring veils of thoughts and words that blinded it to the truth. The forceful and uncompromising stance adopted by both sides led to increasing alienation between the doctrinal and Zen schools. A similar conflict was likewise raging in China at that time, and the basic tension between these two approaches has persisted within the Buddhist community down to the present day.

Hence the ideological unity of Buddhism, which the Silla rulers used as a means to integrate a divided land and which Wonhyo sought to restore through his philosophy of reconciliation, became a distant memory in the final years of the dynasty. As the Silla kingdom neared its end, nine separate schools (the "nine-mountain" sects) stood in opposition to the various doctrinal schools.

THE KORYO DYNASTY (935–1392)

The Silla dynasty was finally overthrown and replaced by the Koryo regime, under the leadership of King T'aejo (r. 918–43). The dynastic change initially proved to be of great advantage to Buddhism. The religion was immediately reaffirmed as a major source of national unity and well-being. The early rulers set about establishing numerous temples with many members of the royalty and aristocracy entering the religious orders. Monasteries were endowed with vast tracts of land and serfs; they were made exempt from taxation and their monks were freed from compulsory state labor or military service. Many priests were solely employed in the recitation of prayers and scriptures to ensure the prosperity of the kingdom and the success of government policies. A special system of examinations was initiated in order to qualify monks for public office. Above all, the belief that the welfare of the state depended to such a large extent upon the maintenance and support of Buddhism prevailed as it never had before. Even the best known cultural achievement of the period, the carving of the enormous Buddhist canon on eighty-thousand woodblocks, was carried out as a means to defend the country against foreign invasion from the north.

Although the relationship between Buddhism and the state in Koryo was similar in many respects to the situation in Silla, there were some important differences. Prior to unification the rulers of Silla had encouraged the practice of Buddhism as a vital element in achieving a united and politically stable country. Thus Buddhism was seen as a dynamic force that inspired people to realize a new and transformed state. Its continued support throughout Silla was always viewed against the background of the productive role it played in establishing the dynasty. During the Koryo period, however, it was conceived in the fundamentally passive role of preserving the status quo. It became a completely integral part of the state bureaucracy, unquestioningly regarded as a necessary ideological component of national stability. Thus, in the minds of many monks, the distinction between the spiritual goals of the religion and the secular aims of the state became blurred. This resulted in an increasing worldliness among the clergy and the growing political and economic power of the monasteries.

The Koryo period existed concurrently with the Song dynasty (960–1297) in China and several of its distinctive features were likewise present there. Zen was one of the only major movements to survive the severe persecutions of Buddhism in 845 intact. It became more widely accepted and moved out of the mountainous regions it had inhabited during the Tang period into the more populated regions of social and cultural activity. Under the inspiration of such figures as Dahui (1089–1163) a rapprochement was undertaken with the doctrinal schools. During this time famous encounters and dialogues between the Tang masters and their disciples were formalized into a system of koans and recorded in such works as the *Blue Cliff Records* (*Biyanlu*). However, throughout the Song dynasty no new major schools of Buddhism emerged. It was a period in which the creative energy of the Tang was absorbed, synthesized, and given artistic and literary expression. Moreover, the original source of Chinese Buddhism finally dried up during this time when the religion was destroyed in India in 1183. All of these factors were either influential or reflected in the development of Buddhism in the Koryo dynasty.

The principal task within the Korean Buddhist community during the entire Koryo period was that of reconciling the disputing factions which had emerged at the end of Silla. The Zen schools could no longer be dismissed as groups of eccentrics and intellectually banished to the safe distance of their mountain centers. They continued to grow in popularity and influence to the point where they began to overshadow the doctrinal schools. By the end of the dynasty, Zen had established itself as the predominant Buddhist movement in the country. However, this predominance was not achieved at the expense of simply undermining the doctrinal schools, but through cultivating a symbiotic relationship in which the practice of Zen was provided with a solid theoretical underpinning.

The first major figure who attempted to harmonize the doctrinal and the Zen groups was the monk Uich'on (1055–1101). The fourth son of King Munjong (r. 1046–83), Uich'on is a good example of an aristocratic and powerful monk of the Koryo dynasty. His father encouraged him to receive ordination at the age of eleven, and for the rest of his life his activities were given the full support of the court. Uich'on was first and foremost a scholar. He was well versed in most of the important Buddhist doctrines prevailing at his time. However, his main interest came to be focused on the teachings of the Tiantai (K. Ch'ont'ae) school.

Tiantai teachings represent an early indigenous Chinese attempt at creating a unified view of the different Buddhist doctrines inherited from India. The Tiantai school was founded in the sixth century by Zhiyi (538–97) and took as its central text the Lotus Sutra. Zhiyi believed that this scripture provided the highest expression of Buddhist doctrine, in relation to which all other views could be graded and systemized. Moreover, it was a school which emphasized the importance of meditation as well as of scriptural study and devotion. Uich'on believed that it was just such a unified view of Buddhism that was needed in Korea to resolve the conflicts between the diverse sects. Although the Tiantai teachings were already known to the Koreans during the Silla period, they never attracted sufficient interest to be formed into an independent school. Thus it was Uich'on who was responsible for bringing the doctrine to the attention of the monks and scholars of Koryo and through his own efforts as well as through official backing he established the school in Korea.

However, Uich'on's goal of reconciliation through the Tiantai teachings was never fully realized. The intrinsic complexity of the Tiantai system, which involved both the detailed classification of scriptures and the grasp of difficult and abstract philosophical concepts, gave the school a strongly intellectual flavour which tended to repel the Zen followers. Moreover, the school's traditional reservations about the iconoclastic Zen teachings as well as Uich'on's own strongly worded criticism of Zen did not serve in the interests of mutual harmony. Although Uich'on's efforts attracted many followers and secured the foundations of a relatively long-lived school, the unity he sought to achieve among the different sects eluded him.

It was not until a hundred or so years after the death of Uich'on that an effective and enduring syncretic vision of Buddhism finally emerged in Korea. This vision was the work of the monk Chinul (1158–1210) who, together with Wonhyo, is considered as one of the greatest figures in the history of Korean Buddhism. Chinul was born at a time of political upheaval and religious deterioration. During the early decades of the twelfth century the kingdom of Koryo was beset with external threats of invasion, internal strife, uprisings, and coups against the court. Both doctrinal and Zen Buddhism had entered a period of enervation and decline.

Chinul began his monastic training when he was seven years old. He received ordination as a novice at fifteen and by the time he was twenty-five had successfully passed the clerical examinations necessary for pursuing a career in the monastic hierarchy. However, he was dismayed by the current degeneration visible in the institutionalized church and renounced all intention to involve himself with it. Consequently, he retreated to the mountains where he spent many years in relative solitude devoting himself to study and contemplation. Although he was formally ordained in one of the Zen schools, it seems that he never developed a close teacher-disciple relationship with any one master. Instead, he remained by himself, cultivating an understanding of Buddhism through his own research into the scriptures and his continuous practice of Zen meditation. Moreover, unlike many of his contemporaries, he never traveled to China to pursue his training.

During this time he experienced three separate spiritual awakenings. The realizations he gained on these occasions were fundamental to the subsequent outlook on Buddhist theory and practice he formulated in his later years. All three experiences occured upon his coming across certain key passages in texts he was studying at the time. On the first occasion he was reading Huineng's Platform Sutra; on the second, Li Tongxuan's *Exposition of the Avatamsaka Sutra;* and on the third, *The Records of Dahui.* In this way the basic compatability of doctrine and Zen was revealed to him through his own personal acceptance and application of both approaches. Unlike Uich'on, his understanding of the harmony between the different schools was not thought out beforehand and then subsequently imposed in the form of a complex intellectual ideology: it emerged naturally from his own practice.

Since he had been a young man, Chinul had dreamt of forming a community of like-minded friends who also wished to separate themselves from the increasing worldliness of institutionalized Buddhism and devote themselves purely to study and meditation. However, his initial attempts were thwarted and it was only in 1190, when he was thirty-two, that he was able to create such a group. They settled at Kojo monastery and called themselves the Concentration and Wisdom Community. For the next seven years they remained in retreat, their number steadily increasing as more and more monks became attracted to their renewed seriousness in the practice of Buddhism. It was then decided to find another location where a larger facility could be created to accommodate the growing community. In the year 1200 Chinul arrived at Mount Chogye where some of his followers were already in the process of enlarging a small hermitage into a sizable monastery complex. The work was completed five years later and the temple came to be known as Songgwang Sa. Chinul settled here for the remaining five years of his life. He taught extensively, led retreats, and completed his two most important works, *Excerpts from the Exposition of the Avatamsaka Sutra* and *Excerpts from the Dharma Collection and Special Practice Record*. His fame spread and he finally gained the respect and patronage of the court that he had initially shunned. He died in 1210 while sitting on his lecture seat discussing points of Dharma with his disciples. After his death he was given the posthumous title of National Master Pojo, by which name he is best known today.

Central to Chinul's thinking is the conviction that the message contained in the Buddhist sutras and the truth transmitted through the experience of awakening in Zen are essentially identical. Thus he saw the conflict and sectarianism of the doctrinal and the Zen schools of his time to be based upon an entirely false distinction. To eliminate this misunderstanding and thereby lay the ground for reconciliation, he primarily drew upon the writings of three somewhat unrelated Chinese teachers: Zongmi (780–841), a Tang Zen master, Avatamsaka patriarch, and advocate of syncretism; Li Tongxuan (635–730), an obscure commentator on the Avatamsaka Sutra; and Dahui, the Song-dynasty systemizer of Zen who died the year before Chinul founded his Concentration and Wisdom Community.

In the works of Zongmi, Chinul found one of his most basic doctrines: the notion of sudden awakening followed by gradual cultivation. This approach to practice stood in sharp contrast to the radical view of some Zen teachers, who maintained that once one awakened to one's fundamental nature, all of one's subsequent actions would spontaneously flow from the naturally pure sphere of enlightenment. Chinul believed that such an initial sudden awakening did not signal the completion of the Buddhist path, but revealed the basis upon which the path could authentically develop and lead to the final purification of inherited defilements and the full actualization of wholesome qualities in Buddhahood. Such a view of Zen practice found complementary support in Li Tongxuan's interpretation of the Avatamsaka Sutra. The Avatamsaka sect, in addition to being the most popular doctrinal school in Korea, had frequently attracted the attention of Zen teachers with its descriptions of the unimpeded interpenetration of all phenomena, a view of reality that resonated most closely with many of their own experiences. Moreover, it presented a detailed step-by-step account of the bodhisattva's progress from the initial stages of faith to final and complete enlightenment. In contrast to other commentators on this sutra, Li Tongxuan maintained that the realization of enlightenment did not only occur after a long and arduous period of time but actually took place in this very life at the *beginning* of the path. On the basis of the initial awakening to the unimpeded interpenetration of all things, the aspirant thereby experiences the presence of full Buddhahood within his own defiled state of mind. This gives him firm confidence in his own essential nature and inspires him to bring that essential nature to complete actuality in Buddhahood.

For Chinul, the sudden awakening experienced through Zen meditation was identical to the initial realization of the unimpeded interpenetration of phenomena described in the Avatamsaka Sutra. The various stages to Buddhahood described in the sutra were a precise account of the gradual cultivation which Zongmi had insisted should succeed the initial sudden awakening. As for a practical means for achieving sudden awakening, Chinul turned to Dahui's explanation of *hwadu* practice. This was a method devised by Southern Song-dynasty Zen teachers as an effective device to awaken to the meaning of the truth transmitted from the first Zen patriarchs. Chinul was the first person to introduce this technique into Korea. Even today it is the predominant method employed by Zen masters in the country.

In both his life and his writings Chinul demonstrated a unified view of the study of doctrine and the practice of Zen, an achievement that was rarely paralleled even in China. He established the basic outlook of Korean Zen Buddhism that has characterized the religion ever since his time. His works form a central part of the present monastic study program and his instructions for meditation are followed in most modern Zen monasteries in Korea. However, he received neither formal confirmation of his awakening nor the transmission vital to the continuity of the Zen lineage. Moreover, his unwillingness to involve himself in the maneuverings of the institutionalized Buddhism of his time and his early death at fifty-two prevented him from being in a position to actually bring about a concrete unification of the different schools.

A final attempt to restore unity among the various Buddhist schools was made during the last decades of the Koryo dynasty by the monk T'aego (1301–82). However, he too proved to be incapable of preventing the further deterioration of Buddhism during this period. Nevertheless, he made two important contributions to the Buddhist community that were to have far-reaching consequences.

T'aego was ordained in the Chogye Zen sect. (This was the name adopted after the time of Chinul by the original Mount Kaji school of Toui. Thus, he was a distant successor of Chinul.) At the age of thirty-seven he experienced a major spiritual awakening after many years of practicing Zen. Nine years later he traveled to China and had his enlightenment confirmed by Jinggong (1272–1352), an eighteenth-generation disciple in the line of the famous Zen master Linji (J. Rinzai; d. 867). In this way the continuity of transmission from the earliest Zen patriarchs, which Chinul lacked, was clearly established in T'aego. For this reason Korean Zen masters down to the present day trace their lineage back to T'aego and regard him as the ancestor of the Korean Zen tradition. The second contribution of T'aego was that of uniting the nine separate Zen sects that had developed at the end of the Silla dynasty. In addition to their disputes with the doctrinal schools, at the close of the Koryo period the nine mountain schools of Zen were also in conflict with one another. With the support of King Kongmin (r. 1352–72), T'aego set about to unify these nine schools into one. This he achieved in 1356. He called the resultant single school the "Chogye" sect—the name the principal Buddhist order of Korea still preserves today.

Ten years after the death of T'aego the Koryo dynasty was overthrown. With its demise the Buddhist church, which had been so closely affiliated to the ruling aristocracy, was likewise discredited. The royal protection and support that had been the cause of the prosperity and power of Buddhism during the dynasty also turned out to be the cause of its downfall.

THE YI DYNASTY (1392–1910)

Although Yi Songgye (r. 1392–98), the founder of the Yi dynasty, was himself a Buddhist, he was unable to tolerate the continued erosion of political and economic power from the state by the monasteries. He also faced considerable pressure from the rising group of Confucianists within the government to impose restrictions upon the Buddhists' activity. Toward the end of the Koryo period, as the economic structure began to collapse, many monasteries and powerful officials took advantage of the confusion to illegally increase their land holdings. Thus the initial criticisms of the Confucianists were made mainly on economic grounds. However, as their influence continued to grow during the Yi dynasty, the arguments between the Confucianists and the Buddhists came to include more basic philosophical and ethical questions. The Confucianists, who had previously been overshadowed by the Buddhists on spiritual issues, owed their new-found inspiration and creativity to a reformed kind of Confucianism that had slowly emerged in China since the eighth century. This "neo-Confucianism" was introduced into Korea in 1290 and steadily grew in influence and popularity, reaching the peak of its development in the mid-sixteenth century.

In China during the Song, Ming (1368–1644), and Qing (1644–1911) dynasties, neo-Confucianism became a predominant spiritual force among the intellectual and governing classes. Buddhism remained relatively strong as a popular religion: the building of temples and the ordination of monks and nuns continued. But it ceased to act as the hub of spiritual and philosophical activity as it had during the Tang epoch. The doctrinal schools largely fell into decline and were replaced with the immensely popular Pure Land sect and, to a lesser degree, by the Zen schools.

As the Yi dynasty progressed, the court steadily shifted its allegiance to the neo-Confucianists. In general this resulted in less and less material support for the Buddhist monasteries as well as an overall movement of interest away from the ideals of Buddhism. On occasion, however, this gradual decline was accelerated by specific acts of repression and persecution. During the early decades of the Yi period several decrees were issued that ordered the limitation in scope of the Buddhist examinations and their replacement with Confucian ones; the restriction of the number of temples and monks within given areas; and the confiscation of the property of the monasteries, as well as the abolition of their tax-exempt status. The principal aim of these measures was to undermine the economic and political power of the Buddhists by disqualifying them from government service, reducing their personnel and depriving them of their wealth. Later kings enforced even more severe restrictions. Buddhist examinations were entirely abolished. From 1623 onwards temples were forbidden in the capital and monks were prohibited from even setting foot there. Buddhist ceremonies were outlawed and replaced with Confucian rites. At one point it was officially made illegal to receive monastic ordination.

Under King Sejong (r. 1419–50) measures were taken to forcibly unite the different Buddhist schools of the time into orders. This resulted in the Chogye Zen sect, the Tiantai, and Vinaya schools being united as the Zen order; and the Avatamsaka, Yogacara, and two other doctrinal schools being merged into one doctrinal order. Although some regard this unification as a positive result of the Korean tendency toward syncretism and harmony, it seems that the move was probably motivated more by political than spiritual concerns. By having only two schools to deal with rather than seven, it was all the easier for the government to oversee and control the activities of Buddhism.

Despite the general anti-Buddhist sentiment that prevailed during the Yi dynasty, certain sympathetic rulers attempted to revive Buddhism and restore some of its previous privileges. In his later years King Sejong became a supporter of Buddhism and even constructed a temple on the grounds of the royal palace. King Sejo (r. 1455–68) was also an ardent Buddhist and went to considerable lengths to try and rehabilitate the religion. However, his efforts were canceled by his next three successors, who initiated an era of persecution that lasted until 1544. The greatest royal supporter of Buddhism to appear was the Queen Mother Munjong, who ruled the country as regent from 1550 to 1565. She reintroduced the Buddhist official hierarchy and government examinations for monks and appointed Houng Pou (d. 1566) as the head of both Buddhist orders. Under the patronage of the queen and the strong leadership of Houng Pou, Buddhism began to recover. But this revival ended with the death of the queen and the exile and assassination of Houng Pou the following year.

It was during this brief period of resuscitation under Queen Munjong that the best-known Buddhist figure of the Yi dynasty, the monk Sosan (1520–1604), emerged. Like most young noblemen of his time Sosan was given a traditional Confucian education. However, he failed the government examinations when he was fifteen and shortly afterward decided to renounce his worldly ambitions and become a Buddhist monk. For many years he lived in the mountainous regions of the country devoting himself to the practice of Zen and study of the scriptures. When he was thirty-one he decided to take the official Buddhist government examinations which had been reinstated the previous year by Queen Munjong. He then entered into government service and in 1566 succeeded Houng Pou as the head official of both the Zen and doctrinal orders. However, two years later he became disillusioned with this kind of work, resigned under the pretext of eye disease, and retreated again to the mountains. For the next thirty-four years he remained in solitude and obscurity.

Sosan was a prolific writer renowned for his mastery of poetry and calligraphy. In his thinking he was primarily concerned with the teachings of Zen, but also emphasized many of the ideas on the unity of Zen and doctrinal study first put forth by Chinul. Through his efforts an interest was rekindled in Zen and the school started to undergo a revival.

However, Sosan is primarily remembered for his remarkable loyalty to his country during the Japanese invasion of 1592 under General Hideyoshi. At this time he was already an old man of seventy-two. Yet upon realizing the extent of the Japanese advance he took it upon himself to organize the Buddhist monks into a militia unit to fight the Japanese. He received the full support of the king and was authorized to encourage the conscription of monks throughout the country. These units played a significant role in the defeat of the Japanese army in 1598. For his part Sosan was given the highest honors by the king and many shrines and memorials were erected to his memory. However, the official attitude toward the Buddhist community as a whole remained unchanged and the same policy of suppression was continued. The idea of a monk militia was nevertheless preserved, and in 1627 and 1637 the unit was used to defend the capital from the invading Mongolian forces from the north. Even today all Buddhist monks in Korea are obliged to perform military service.

After the death of Sosan in 1604 no outstanding Buddhist teacher emerged for over two hundred and fifty years until the final decades of the Yi dynasty. Only under the rule of King Chongjo (1777–1800) and King Kojong (1864–

1906) was any effort made to encourage the revival of Buddhism. Throughout this long period the Zen and doctrinal schools were forced to restrict their activities to outlying rural districts. Very often their temples became centers for popular devotion among the country people. The monasteries and hermitages were also used as places of retreat from the pressures of the world by Confucian scholars and officials. In this way a certain contact was maintained between the ruling aristocracy and the Buddhist heritage of the previous dynasties. Yet despite their isolated and discredited position, the Buddhists succeeded in keeping their traditions alive and transmitting this knowledge from one generation to the next.

The final years of the Yi period during the latter half of the nineteenth century were a time of great change, confusion, and turmoil in the countries of East Asia. The dynasties that had ruled for centuries in both China and Korea gradually lost their vitality and became ossified, corrupt regimes only interested in preserving their own power. Neo-Confucianism had decayed from a progressive spiritual movement into a dogmatic and ineffectual political ideology. Moreover, the traditional values of Chinese society were beginning to be challenged from all sides by increasingly powerful influences from Europe and America. Christianity was already established in China and Korea and active missionary work was under way. The radically new world-view of science was also making itself felt. Progressive ideas of democracy and social reform were starting to attract the attention of the young and disaffected. The Western powers were insistently demanding trade agreements and diplomatic relations with the Asian countries. Finally, in 1876, Korea abolished its policy of isolation and opened its doors to the world community.

King Kojong, the last major ruler of the Yi period, tried in several ways to reestablish the dignity of Buddhism during these decades of crisis. At the very beginning of his reign he released the monasteries from their heavy tax burdens and exempted monks from compulsory state labor. In April 1895 he finally lifted the ban on monks entering the capital and allowed the reconstruction of temples. In the following year a conference was held in Seoul in which Korean and Japanese Buddhists met to discuss the future of Buddhism in Korea. This resulted in permission being given to the Japanese to start wide-scale missionary work in the country. In 1899 a central office for all Buddhist sects in Korea was established in the capital. These measures were partly responsible for creating the foundations of a renewed and independent Buddhist identity which, in its embryonic stages, was soon confronted with the modern world.

THE MODERN ERA (1910–)

In 1911 the Qing dynasty collapsed and was replaced by the Republic of China. On August 29th of the previous year Japan had forcibly annexed Korea and placed the country under Japanese sovereignty. Korea remained under colonial rule, during which time the people had to struggle to retain their national, cultural, and religious identity. However, the Japanese movement toward annexation may have actually begun as early as 1877, as soon as the Koreans permitted a foreign presence on their soil. To prepare the ground for the eventual political domination of the country, the Japanese attempted to win the sympathy of the people through the propagation of Japanese Buddhism. The first Japanese temple was founded in Pusan in 1877, ostensibly to serve the Japanese community. By the time of annexation, six different Japanese sects—including the nationalistic Nichiren school and various Pure Land traditions—had established about one hundred and eighty temples throughout the country. Moreover, on the grounds that they wished to revitalize Buddhism in Korea, leaders of several Japanese schools had attempted to gain control of the Korean monasteries by merging them into their own schools. Yet they met with little success.

As soon as Korea came under complete Japanese rule in 1910, the administration of the Buddhist orders was taken over by an office of the occupation government. At this time several Koreans began to feel that their own form of Buddhism would be unable to survive at all unless it were in some way unified with one of the Japanese sects. Most prominent among these men was Yi Hoegwang, the current leader of the Korean Buddhist schools. He was convinced by representatives of the Japanese Soto Zen sect that since Korean Buddhism was also primarily a Zen school, it would be more reasonable to seek a merger with another Zen sect than with either the Nichiren or Pure Land schools. Yi went to Japan in 1910 and secretly conferred with the leaders of the Soto sect. Although he insisted on a merger of equal standing between the Korean and Japanese schools, the agreement was clearly weighted in favor of the Japanese. On returning to Korea he presented his plan and initially won considerable support among Korean monks. However, his agreement was denounced as a sell-out by many important Buddhist leaders and, in 1911, the government refused to endorse the plan on the grounds that it would only divide the Korean Buddhists.

There now followed a period of considerable confusion. The Korean Zen and doctrinal schools both realized that they were in danger of being absorbed into a Japanese sect but they still lacked sufficient unity to be able to indefinitely resist the pressures of the occupying power. After the return of Ti Hoegwang from Japan, the Zen school had now split into two factions. Yet the increasing oppression of the Japanese government gave rise to strong anti-Japanese sentiments throughout the Buddhist community. To a large extent it was the shared feelings toward a common enemy that served as the driving force in achieving a unified church.

In 1921 a group of young monks organized the "Buddhist Reform Society" and put forward demands for a central, Korean-controlled body with authority over all major temples in the country. After three years of factional disputes and conflict with the Japanese, this was finally established, but it lacked any real executive power. Subsequent conferences in 1928 and 1929 resulted in further progress toward the institution of reforms, independence from Japanese control, and the harmonization of the Zen and doctrinal schools. Finally, in 1935, agreement was reached on the unification of both major schools into the single Chogye order. In 1941 the occupation government changed its policy concerning the Korean Buddhists and officially authorized the school. From independence four years later until the present day, the unified Chogye order has remained the dominant force within Korean Buddhism.

On the positive side, the pressures of the Japanese occupation forced the weak and alienated Buddhism at the end of the Yi dynasty to assert itself as a unified tradition with its own unique identity. The Koreans were motivated to rediscover the strong points of their religion, which had been forged during the Silla and Koryo dynasties. This brought to the fore once again the spirit of reconciliation that had characterized Buddhism throughout its history in Korea. By the end of the Japanese occupation, Korean Buddhism was a unified and revitalized religion with its headquarters situated in the heart of the capital.

The Japanese presence also had certain disruptive effects upon the Buddhist community. Under the influence of the married Japanese priests in the country, some Korean monks began to relax their rule of celibacy and likewise took wives and started families. This became an increasingly popular practice and by the 1930s many temples throughout the land were run by married "monks." Consequently, the monasteries began to lose their traditional lay supporters and, in addition, were obliged to provide for the families of the priests. After independence, the Chogye order insisted on the celibate status of its monks and dismissed many married priests from positions of authority in the temples. This latter move gave rise to a great deal of conflict between the celibate and noncelibate factions. The problem became so serious that in 1954 President Syngman Rhee had to intervene to resolve the dispute. Nowadays, the celibate Chogye order controls the majority of temples in the country but some remain under the administration of noncelibate orders.

The most significant Buddhist teacher at the outset of the modern era was undoubtedly the monk Kyongho (1849–1912). He was primarily responsible for reviving the spirit of the Zen school both through his teachings and living example. After many years of study and meditation he underwent a major awakening at thirty-two. This was confirmed by Master Yongam, an eleventh-generation successor of Sosan, who then gave him the transmission. From this time on he taught throughout the country and became widely known and respected. At the age of fifty-two he went to Haein Sa monastery to supervise a new publication of the Buddhist canon. But the following year he disappeared from public view, retired to a small village, wore lay clothes, and grew his hair long. Until his death nine years later he followed this eccentric way of life, instructing whoever he happened to meet.

Kyongho had several important disciples: the illiterate and outwardly simple Hyewol (1861–1937); the politically active monk Yongsong (1864–1937), who was involved both in establishing monastic farming communities and translating Buddhist sutras into the Korean vernacular script; the well-known teacher Mangong (1872–1946); and Hanam (1876–1951) who chose to remain in his hermitage and die rather than flee from the Communist forces during the Korean war. It was largely through the efforts of Kyongho and his disciples that Zen Buddhism was reestablished as an active spiritual movement in modern Korea after its long period of stagnation during the Yi dynasty. Many of the Zen masters alive today trace their immediate lineage back to Kyongho and draw upon his teachings for inspiration.

Independence from Japanese rule in 1945 was followed six years later by the Korean War, which resulted, in 1953, in the division of the country into the Communist-controlled north and non-Communist south. Although it is difficult to obtain any exact information, it is assumed that since then Buddhism has been completely suppressed in North Korea. The postwar era in South Korea has witnessed a tremendous increase in religious activity. Much of this has come in the wake of the remodeling of the country along Western economic and social lines. South Korea has become a rapidly expanding industrial nation. This has resulted in the increasing urbanization of the population, an almost exclusive emphasis on Western standards of education, and a burgeoning middle class. This mixture of social upheaval and Westernization has proved to be an exceptionally fertile ground for Christian missionary work. Over the last thirty years Christianity has become the fastest growing and, in many respects, the most visible religious movement. Buddhism has nevertheless maintained a solid and well-established presence. There are an estimated eight million Buddhists in the country served by around fifteen thousand ordained monks and nuns.

On looking back at the history of Buddhism in Korea over the past seventeen hundred years one observes a religion that throughout its various phases has continuously influenced and shaped the minds and culture of the Korean people. It has served to unify the country politically as well as spiritually and has produced a number of exceptional Buddhist teachers. Its ability to survive nearly six hundred years of repression under a hostile Confucian dynasty further indicates that its roots run deep into the spiritual foundations of Korean society. Yet the years of suppression under the Yi rulers and the Japanese occupation, together with the decline of Buddhism in China, have inevitably weakened the religion. In addition, it is now faced with the challenging task of establishing itself as a relevant and meaningful religion capable of dealing with the spiritual crises of the twentieth century. No longer does it enjoy the unqualified support of the state, yet neither is it subject to suppressive and restrictive measures. For the first time in its history it finds itself in a pluralistic society informed by conflicting and competing religious outlooks each with equal freedom to express and assert its beliefs. Although Buddhism has the advantage of being a tradition rooted in the cultural history of Korea, it has the disadvantage of often being perceived as belonging to a past that is rapidly being left behind. Thus its future will to a large extent depend upon the ways in which the tradition can come to terms with the present situation and in which the present generation succeeds in appropriating its heritage from the past.[1]

CHAPTER TWO

Songgwang Sa: Life in
a Korean Zen Monastery

THE PRINCIPAL Buddhist monasteries existing in
Korea today are usually one of two kinds. They either serve as centers for the study of the Buddhist scriptures
or they provide facilities for Zen meditation. Some of the
larger monasteries accommodate both possibilities: one
section being used for studying the sutras and another en-
closed area housing a hall for meditation. Since the unification of the Zen and doctrinal schools into the single Chogye
order, the kind of training pursued in any particular monastery no longer indicates an affiliation to a certain sect.
The monasteries are governed by a single administrative
body that oversees the activities of all these different study
and meditation centers. In addition to the large training
monasteries, which are usually located in quiet and remote
areas, there are numerous small temples in villages and towns
throughout the country that attend to the needs of the
Buddhist laity.

Once a young monk has completed a postulancy period
of several months and received ordination as a novice, he is
encouraged to enter either a sutra school or a meditation
hall. If he chooses the former, he may embark on a training
period of up to six years, during which time he is primarily
engaged in the study of Buddhist scriptures. These texts

are mainly comprised of Mahayana sutras, records of well-known Zen masters, and instructions in monastic life. The scriptures are studied in classical Chinese with lectures and explanations given in Korean. If he chooses the latter alternative, he enters a meditation hall and devotes himself to the practice of Zen. It is also quite common for monks to go to a meditation hall after completing their training in scriptural study. This procedure is the same for nuns as well as for monks.

Among the various meditation monasteries in Korea, a monk may decide to undertake his training at Songgwang Sa. This monastery is situated in the southwest corner of the country in the province of Cholla Namdo, between the towns of Kwangju and Suncheon. It was established in its present form at the beginning of the thirteenth century by Chinul as the place to settle his Concentration and Wisdom Community. It has continued to serve as a major center for the practice of Zen ever since.

Songgwang Sa is reached by a narrow, unpaved road that winds gently up from the valley below. The monastery itself is nestled in a circle of steep, forested hills, insulated by nature from the disturbances of the outside world. Nearby, a clear stream weaves its way between boulders and tumbles down the mountainside. When Chinul arrived here in 1200, he was immediately impressed by the suitability of the place for establishing a meditation community. A record of the Koryo period remarks that "the site was outstanding and the land fertile; the springs were sweet and the forests abundant. It was truly a place which would be appropriate for cultivating the mind, nourishing the nature, gathering an assembly and making merit."[2]

The monastery complex itself is formed around a spacious, square courtyard. Dominating this open space is the main Buddha hall, an impressive wooden structure mounted with an imposing yet delicate Chinese-style slate roof. As with most of the temple buildings in the monastery, its walls are colorfully decorated with figures from the Buddhist pantheon, scenes from the lives of famous monks, and landscapes; the ceiling is adorned with a profusion of multicolored, interweaving patterns and motifs. Around the central courtyard are smaller temples of similar design dedicated to different bodhisattvas. There are also a dining and a kitchen area, living quarters for the monks, and rooms for guests.

Immediately behind the main Buddha hall, and elevated some fifty feet upon the hillside, lies another group of buildings. This is where the meditation hall, a large lecture room, a couple of small temples, and the quarters of the Zen master are located. The area is sealed off from the rest of the monastery and is only accessible to those monks undergoing training in Zen meditation. It overlooks the entire monastery and offers a panoramic view of the surrounding hills and mountains.

Once a monk has been formally accepted into the community, he then moves into the meditation hall and installs what few possessions he has in a locker. According to the length of time he has been ordained, he is assigned a place in one of the two rows of meditation cushions that run down the length of the hall. This is where he will sit facing the wall in meditation during the day and lie down to sleep at night. The hall is uncluttered and spacious. The walls and ceiling are white. In the middle of the long back wall is a small altar above which hangs a mirror symbolizing the true mind that the monks seek to realize. The floor is covered with varnished, yellow-ochre paper and is heated from below by a wood fire. The doors are just sliding paper screens. During the day the room is illuminated by soft, natural light that filters through the paper doors. After dusk a dull electric lamp is used. The hall is suffused with an atmosphere of peace and simplicity. There are a minimum of external objects to distract the monk from his meditation.

Each year is divided into four periods. Two three-month sessions during summer and winter are devoted to intensive Zen training. At these times, the monks must follow a strict group schedule and are not allowed to leave the monastery grounds. During spring and autumn, though, the formal schedule is relaxed. Those who wish to can remain in the meditation hall and continue their practice; the others are free to travel to different temples and hermitages throughout the country. Few of the monks commit themselves indefinitely to one particular meditation hall. At the end of each season most of the meditators disperse. The following season a new group is formed. The tradition of wandering monks with no fixed home is still maintained in Korea.

Each day of the three-month meditation period follows an identical pattern that is decided upon by the thirty or so monks who gather before the season formally begins. This pattern is broken only for the fortnightly head-shaving and bathing day, which is followed the next morning by the recitation of the monastic precepts and that afternoon by a discourse from the Zen master. Occasionally, if there is work to be done in the monastery's fields, the monks interrupt their schedule to partake in whatever manual labor is required of them.

The day begins at three o'clock, with a short service consisting of three bows before the altar. The monks then take their places in the rows of cushions and the first period of meditation is announced with three strikes of a wooden clapper. Fifty-minute sittings are broken with ten-minute sessions of walking briskly around the hall. This schedule of sitting alternated with walking continues throughout the day until nine or ten o'clock at night. Two or three one-hour breaks are taken for the three daily meals, during which time the monks can also rest and go for short walks in the surrounding hills. Before the midday meal, the entire community assembles in the main Buddha hall for a service, chanting, and the formal offering of rice to the

Buddha. When the service is over, they walk in single file to the nearby dining hall and take their places—again, assigned according to how long they have been ordained.

All three meals of the day are basically identical. The same silent procedure—each monk setting out his four bowls wrapped in cloth; being served water, rice, and soup; taking various pickled vegetables and soy products from side trays; and, finally, rinsing and cleaning the bowls after eating—is followed morning, noon, and evening. Each phase in the procedure is signaled by a number of strikes from a wooden clapper. At lunchtime, the meal is taken wearing formal robes and is accompanied by various prayers. When the meal is over not a grain of rice nor a drop of water remains on the floor. The bowls are again neatly wrapped and placed upon a shelf above each monk's place. The meditators then return to the hall where they may drink a cup of tea or milk and eat some fruit before resuming their practice.

While sitting in the hall the monk is expected to quietly concentrate on his *hwadu* and avoid making any noise or movement which might disturb the others. During the long, regulated hours of meditation he is forced to tackle drowsiness, boredom, distracted thoughts, and fantasies. He has to bear terrible pains in his legs, his back, and shoulders. Unlike in some Japanese temples, in Korean monasteries there is no disciplinarian pacing back and forth with a stick to enforce a straight sitting posture. Nor is the practice one which demands that the student "pass" a series of many koans. Although he may seek the advice of the Zen master and elder meditators, the monk must rely on his own inner determination and resolve to overcome the hardships of sitting and the sometimes oppressive monotony of penetrating to the heart of a single koan.

Every two weeks, on the days of the full and the new moons, the monks assemble in the lecture hall to hear a formal discourse from the Zen master. After chanting some verses of prayer, the monks wait for the teacher to ascend the "Dharma seat" and then they bow to him three times. The Dharma seat is raised three or four feet above the floor. In front of it is a lectern upon which the master places his terse written text. A candle burns at each corner and to one side a young attendant places a cup of tea. The master sits still for a few moments and observes the monks seated before him. He is dressed in his formal robes and holds a gnarled, brown staff in his right hand.

The discourse begins. The master reads from the Chinese characters of his handwritten text. The lecture is interspersed with verses which are chanted in a peculiarly quivering and undulating rhythm. Periodically, this formal part of the discourse is punctuated by a shout, the striking of the staff upon the base of the seat, or a stony silence as the master slowly looks around him for a response to a question he has just asked. Once the formal lecture has been completed, the master proceeds to give some further explanation on the meaning of the text. This may include his relating a story from the scriptures, elaborating a point in a more understandable manner, or illuminating certain aspects of the meditation practice. Occasionally, a monk will engage the master in a dialogue and try to demonstrate the degree of his understanding. But such attempts are usually dismissed with an even more baffling remark thrown back at the student. In addition to these fortnightly discourses, informal talks are sometimes held in the meditation hall itself. On these occasions the master may recount an episode from his own training or answer questions the monks have about their practice.

Whenever a monk wishes to see the Zen master in private to discuss some aspect of his practice, he is encouraged to visit the master in his quarters. He may then report on the progress or hardships he is experiencing in his meditation and receive advice on how to proceed. Sometimes the monks are called one by one to the master's room in order to formally give an account of their practice. However, regular interviews at which the master keeps a close check on the progress of the student's meditation are not common in the Korean tradition.

As a monk's Zen training progresses, he may place himself more and more under the guidance of a teacher with whom he feels a particular affinity. Nevertheless, he will probably continue traveling around the country and settling in a different meditation hall for the summer and winter retreats. At the end of each retreat he will first of all go to see his teacher to pay his respects and discuss his practice with him. There is no fixed period of training. The itinerant life of wandering from one Zen monastery to another might continue for many years. Yet as he grows older and more established in his practice, a monk might retire to a smaller hermitage away from the formal training atmosphere of the large meditation monasteries. Eventually, as his understanding deepens, he may attract disciples of his own and be required to impart to others the wisdom he has gained from his years of seasoned meditation.

CHAPTER THREE

Master Kusan:
A Biographical Sketch

K USAN SUNIM was born near the small country
town of Namwon in Cholla Bukto, a province in
the southwest of Korea, in 1909. His parents owned a
medium-sized farm, and family life was centered around
work in the fields. Although his parents were Buddhist,
he attended classes at the local Confucian school, where
he studied the Chinese classics, until he was about fifteen.
Upon leaving school, he continued to help on the family
farm and worked as a barber until the age of twenty-nine.
He was also married during this time.

From an early age he had periodically been drawn to
the monastic way of life: "When I was nine years old I
remember thinking, 'Could it be possible for someone to
be without birth and death? Was it possible to have un-
limited powers to move freely through the sky and on the
earth?' Such thoughts made me want to go and live with
the monks in the mountains. But the fear of missing my
parents prevented me from leaving home then. When I
was twenty I also considered such a life. But I was not suf-
ficiently determined."

At the age of twenty-six he was stricken by a severe
illness that caused him a great deal of pain. Upon seeing
him in this condition, a friend who was also a devout Bud-

dhist layman asked him, "Since the abode of the self-nature is originally pure, where does your illness lie?" These words had a deep effect on Master Kusan. Thereupon, he decided to go to Yongwon Sa monastery on Mount Chiri to recite the mantra of Avalokitesvara, *Om mani padme hum,* for one hundred days. Upon completing this period of recitation, he found himself cured of his illness. This experience also served to strengthen greatly his faith in Buddhism.

Three years later, he became convinced that he should dedicate his life to the full-time practice of the teaching of the Buddha. To realize this aim, he left his home and family and started traveling to various monasteries in order to find a teacher. After visiting eleven different temples, he finally came to Songgwang Sa, where he met Hyobong Sunim and was immediately convinced that this master would be a good teacher for him. From that time on he decided to devote himself to the practice of Zen.

Master Hyobong was one of the most remarkable Buddhist teachers of this century in Korea. He was born in 1888 near Pyongyang, which is now the capital of North Korea. As a young man he studied law, and during the Japanese occupation he was the first Korean who was permitted to become a judge. Since many Koreans strongly resisted the Japanese rule, he was often forced to pass judgement on fellow countrymen accused of anti-Japanese activities. This became an increasing source of conflict for him. After he had been a judge for ten years, a case came up in which he was forced to sentence the prisoner to death. The passing of this judgement caused him to question deeply what rights he had to impose punishment on. others. He began to doubt the validity of the entire legal system and the society that supported it. One day he decided that he could no longer continue in such a position. Without telling anyone, he suddenly left his work and home and became a wandering toffee seller.

For the next three years he drifted through the country

barely supporting himself by selling toffee. All this time he reflected upon how he could lead a true and honest human life. He finally decided to enter a monastery and start practicing meditation.

He was already thirty-nine years old when he received ordination. This relatively late start in the monastic life impelled him to practice with especially great earnestness and perseverance. For many years he stayed in retreat concentrating solely on resolving the *hwadu* "No!" When he was forty-three, he built himself a tiny hermitage and sealed himself inside. He left just one small hole in the wall through which food could be passed in and out. For one and a half years he remained in complete solitude. Finally, his mind's eye opened and he realized that at last all of his doubts had been resolved. As an expression of his awakening he wrote the following lines:

At the bottom of the ocean, a deer hatches
    an egg in a swallow's nest.
In the heart of a fire, a fish boils tea in
    a spider's web.
Who knows what is happening in this house?
White clouds float westward; the moon rises
    in the east.

During the next thirty years, Master Hyobong became a widely known and respected teacher. He was eventually appointed the spiritual head of the Chogye order.

Upon meeting Master Hyobong, Kusan Sunim told him that he wished to become a monk and asked him to take him as his disciple. Master Hyobong agreed and instructed him in the *hwadu* "No!" Eight months later he received *sramanera* ordination and entered the meditation hall in Songgwang Sa under the guidance of his teacher. At the age of thirty-one, he went to T'ongdo Sa monastery and took full ordination as a *bhiksu*.

From the beginning, Master Kusan was only interested in the practice of Zen and never attended a sutra school to study the Buddhist scriptures. "I chose to enter the Zen sect because I thought that through meditation I would be able to free myself from birth and death and gain the power to transform this world into a Buddha realm. In the sutra schools, one is only told about cultivating the mind and awakening. I felt it would be better to actually realize these things instead."

As soon as he took up the practice of meditation, he did so with a tremendous resolve and determination. "When I started meditating I was firmly convinced that I would be able to complete the practice within the three months [of the first retreat period]. I exerted myself to the point where I no longer cared whether I lived or died. But as the three months drew to an end, and I had still not realized my goal, I wanted to die, since I felt it was no longer worth living. Once, while doing standing meditation in order to prevent drowsiness, I thought of drowning myself or throwing myself off a high cliff. But at that very moment a huge snow-capped mountain appeared before me. This made me recollect that the Buddha had practiced for six full years at the feet of such mountains. I then realized that it was somewhat presumptuous for me to want to complete my training in three months. Thereupon I renounced my intention to die and redoubled my efforts."

During the following years Kusan Sunim continued to pursue his practice of meditation. After spending a number of seasons in meditation halls, he decided that he needed the solitude of a hermitage in order to be able to concentrate himself fully on his practice. Thus he would spend his time in small remote hermitages often completely by himself. "At these times, when I was hungry, I would find something to eat; when thirsty, I would drink; when the room was cold, I would light a fire under the floor. I tried to practice as hard as I could and would sleep very little."

His disciples recall that in those days Master Kusan was a very stern and even frightening figure. He would demand exemplary conduct from all the younger students of his teacher and urge them to work hard all day and meditate through the night. He would constantly remind them that they never knew when they might die, that they would be finished should the mere breath in their nostrils come to a stop. If a young monk were to waste a few grains of rice or a single cabbage leaf, as a punishment he would sometimes make him go without food for the rest of the day. He himself was a devoted disciple to his teacher and a tireless worker.

His first important experience in meditation came while he was practicing at Sudo Am hermitage. It occurred after he had been meditating continuously for seven days with the intense resolve to awaken before the memorial ceremony for a close friend who had recently died.[3] However, he did not consider this a true awakening. "While meditating such experiences sometimes happen. You could say it was a certain opening of the mind's eye. It was the transition over a difficult step that enabled me to first gain admittance to the door. . . . Perhaps you could call it an initial breakthrough. It showed that my practice was progressing well."

He then went to Popwang Dae, a small hermitage that he had built near Haein Sa monastery, where his teacher was then residing as the Zen Master. He stayed there for three years, and in 1946 he experienced another major breakthrough. This occurred after he had entered a state in which for fifteen days he lost any sense of the outside world. He was no longer concerned whether he lived or died. He was so absorbed in his meditation that birds would come and sit on his head and shoulders and take pieces of stuffing that protruded from his padded coat for their nests. After this, he came down to the main temple in Haein Sa and delivered a formal Dharma discourse to the monks.

He recorded his experience in the following stanza:

> Look at the front of the mirror: it is com-
>   pletely dark.
> Look at the back and it is brilliantly clear.
> Looking at the front, it is not the front;
> Looking at the back, it is also not the back.
> When both front and back are shattered,
> Then truly one has a great complete mirror.

Shortly after the outbreak of the Korean war, Communist forces overran Haein Sa and took all the monks prisoner. Kusan Sunim and Master Hyobong managed to avoid capture and escaped to the region around Pusan where U.N. forces were in control. Master Kusan initially stayed at Ungsok Sa temple and later moved to the nearby town of Chungmu to live in a small temple there until the end of the war. Meanwhile, his teacher had settled at Kumjong Sa, and it was there that Master Kusan received the first formal confirmation of his understanding. On that occasion, he presented this verse:

> The diverse forms in the universe are
>   fundamentally empty—
> So what meaning would there be in pointing
>   at space?
> A withered tree standing on a rock feels
>   neither hot nor cold.
> In spring, flowers bloom; in autumn,
>   fruits are borne.

Master Hyobong replied,

> I planted the stump of a plum tree:
> Due to the old wind, flowers have already
>   blossomed.

Without fail, you will behold the bearing
  of fruit:
Therefore, bring me the pit of the plum!

Being a conscientious member of the Sangha, Master Kusan
was always aware of his wider obligations to the Buddhist
community in Korea. After the war he accepted a number
of administrative positions in order to assist in the regene-
ration of the Buddhist order. He was responsible for the
founding of Milae Sa temple near Chungmu and was
abbot there from 1954 to 1957. At the same time he was
made chief inspector at the National Sangha Headquarters
in Seoul and later head of general monastic affairs in Cholla
Namdo province. He divided his time between these three
jobs.

However, he still felt that his practice of meditation
needed to be deepened. Therefore, he eventually resigned
his posts and went to a small hermitage called Paegun Am.
After meditating there for three years he underwent another
awakening. Upon reporting this to Master Hyobong, who
was then residing in a hermitage near Milae Sa, he received
Dharma transmission. At that time he composed these
lines:

Penetrating deep into a pore of Samantabhadra,
Manjusri is seized and defeated: now the great
  earth is quiet.
It is hot on the day of the winter equinox. Pine
  trees are of themselves green.
A stone man, riding on a crane, passes over the
  blue mountains.

In response, Master Hyobong said, "Until now you have
been following me; now it is I who should follow you."
  In 1962, at the request of his teacher, he came out of
retreat and accepted the position of abbot at Tonghwa Sa

monastery where Master Hyobong was currently the Zen teacher. He remained there for four years. In January 1966, he went abroad for the first time in order to attend an International Buddhist Sangha conference in Sri Lanka. Although he was finally unable to reach his destination, his journey gave him the opportunity to make a pilgrimage to a number of Buddhist holy places in Southeast Asia, India, and Nepal.

Not long after his return, in September of the same year, Master Hyobong passed away in the meditation posture while staying at P'yoch'ung Sa monastery. Shortly before he died he uttered his final, Nirvana poem:

> All my words of Dharma were superfluous.
> You ask me about today's matter—
> I tell you that the moon is shining over
> a thousand rivers.

His remains were distributed to three different temples, Songgwang Sa, P'yoch'ung Sa, and Milae Sa, where they were enshrined in reliquaries. In addition, a stele describing his life was erected to his memory in Songgwang Sa.

The following year Master Kusan moved to Songgwang Sa. Two years later, in 1969, when the monastery became a ch'ongnim (a quasi-autonomous monastic complex incorporating all the different features of Buddhist study and practice), he was instated as the spiritual director of the community, receiving the title Pangjang Sunim. One of his main tasks at that time was the rebuilding of Suson Sa, the principal meditation hall, and the reestablishment of regular Zen training sessions. In 1970 the work was completed and Suson Sa was officially opened.

At the conclusion of his inaugural speech on this occasion, Master Kusan exhorted the monks who were present with these characteristic words of advice: "In practicing meditation you should be prepared to grab hold of the blade of a sword so sharp that it cuts through hairs merely blown against it. You would normally be apprehensive even to take hold of such a sword by its handle since at the slightest slip you would be in danger of cutting yourself. Now you have to be prepared to seize it by the blade! Could you possibly do that in your ordinary frame of mind? As long as you are afraid of the sharpness of the blade you are bound to cut yourself. But in firmly gripping the blade with an utterly intrepid mind, you will not even be scratched."

In 1972 he made his first visit to the United States in order to inaugurate Sambo Sa temple in Carmel, California. At this time he met his first foreign disciple, who subsequently returned with him to Korea. Shortly afterwards he established the Bul-il International Meditation Center in order that the growing number of foreign monks and nuns interested in the practice of Korean Zen Buddhism would be able to follow a traditional training. For this purpose, the Munsu Jon compound within Songgwang Sa was turned over for the use of foreign monks while foreign nuns were housed in a smaller compound on the edge of the main monastery complex. Since then around fifty foreigners from all parts of the world have undergone Zen training in Songgwang Sa. In 1976, *Nine Mountains,* a collection of Master Kusan's teachings translated into English by his foreign disciples, was published privately in Seoul.

Throughout the seventies, Master Kusan worked tirelessly to develop the Zen training facilities at Songgwang Sa. He would preside over both the three-month summer and winter retreats each year, giving formal Dharma lectures and individual instruction. In spite of his age and other responsibilities he would always participate in any manual work in which the other monks were engaged. In addition, he was constantly being invited to give lectures, perform ceremonies, and attend meetings in temples throughout Korea. During his later years, the wrathful demeanor for which he was noted earlier in his life gave way to a kind and compassionate nature that always seemed to have room for any monk or layperson who was in need of his advice.

In the autumn of 1980, he paid a second visit to the United States. He stayed there for five months, during which time he inaugurated Korea Sa temple in Los Angeles as the first foreign branch-temple of Songgwang Sa. He also lectured extensively at Buddhist centers and universities on both the East and West coasts. In the summer of 1982, he was again invited abroad. After a short stay in California, where he founded Taekak Sa in Carmel, he traveled for the first time to Europe. There he lectured in Paris, Geneva, and Copenhagen. In Geneva, he established another small temple, Bulsung Sa.

Master Kusan started to show signs of illness in September of 1983. On October the third he told one of his disciples to write down his Nirvana poem:

> The autumn leaves covering the mountain are
>   redder than flowers in spring.
> Everything in the universe fully reveals
>   the great power.
> Life is void and death is also void.
> Absorbed in the Buddha's ocean-seal samadhi,
>   I depart with a smile.

The following day he gathered his disciples in his room and indicated that he would not live for much longer. From this point on his health gradually deteriorated. He confined himself to his quarters in Songgwang Sa and in the evening of December sixteenth quietly passed away in the meditation posture. Three days before he died, he uttered his final words of Dharma:

> Samsara and Nirvana are originally not two;
> As the sun rises in the sky
> It illuminates the three thousand worlds.

His body was cremated in a small field behind the monastery. After the cremation his disciples examined the remains and discovered fifty-three *sarira* relics. His bones were ground to powder and scattered near the site of his old hermitage at the foot of Mount Chogye.

CHAPTER FOUR

Some Remarks on the Text

IN APPROACHING *The Essential Teachings of the Stone Lion,* one should always bear in mind the purpose of such instructions. The discourses and advice are given exclusively to people who are engaged in the practice of Zen—in most cases, to monks undergoing the Zen training at Songgwang Sa monastery. Thus, the aim of the instructions is solely that of furthering the student's practice of meditation. They are not designed to present an intellectually conceived philosophical attitude through the analysis of which one can then logically infer certain abstract truths. As long as one tries merely to reconstruct a certain philosophic intent lying behind the master's words, one will inevitably miss the point completely. To grasp the import of these teachings, it is essential to open oneself to the inexpressible truth to which these words merely serve as pointers. To cling to the words, the concepts, and their interrelations is to concern oneself with the finger rather than the moon at which it points.

Despite these warnings about the inadequacies of language, it would nevertheless be helpful, especially for those unfamiliar with the terminology of Zen, to say a few words about some of the principal terms which continuously recur in Master Kusan's teachings. Certain concepts are used in a variety of different ways depending upon the context and some take on meanings that are not often found in traditional Indian Buddhism. Since such usage may give rise to misunderstanding, I shall now try to broadly qualify and interpret some of the more important terms.

HWADU (C. *Huatou*). This term, which is used to describe the form of meditation taught by Master Kusan, literally means "head of speech." "Head" here refers to the apex or the point at which speech and thought are exhausted.[4] Thus *hwadu* meditation is aimed at bringing one to a state of clarity and tranquility of mind in which the obscuring and distracting activities of mental chatter are stilled. As a means to reach this state one is instructed to focus the attention upon a question, such as "What is this?" Throughout the text, the term *hwadu* usually refers to the particular question itself as well as the state of mind to be cultivated through concentrating upon the question. Moreover, the term *hwadu* is also used as a virtual synonym for the Japanese term koan (K. *kong an*). Technically speaking, though, these terms differ in meaning. A koan—literally a "public case"—is a description of an entire situation, usually of a dialogue between a Zen master and his disciple; the *hwadu* is only the central point of the exchange which is then singled out as a topic for meditation.[5]

QUESTIONING (K. *uisim;* C. *i xin*). Although this term is usually translated as "doubt," in the context of *hwadu* meditation I feel that "questioning" is more appropriate. Doubt tends to imply either uncertainty, indecision, or vacillation. It is understood as primarily intellectual in character and to occur in the face of making a decision, in having to choose one alternative instead of another. This kind of doubt is not what is to be developed through *hwadu* practice. One of the basic aims of concentrating on a *hwadu* is to sustain a constant sense of inquiry into a question. It is this inquiry or questioning that becomes the inner dynamics of the entire process. But this can only be understood as doubt in the sense that one is faced with a seemingly insoluble problem and does not know how to proceed. Under normal circumstances, doubt is resolved through realizing a particular alternative to be correct or at least the most viable. In *hwadu* meditation, however, the questioning or doubt is resolved in an entirely unforeseeable way. This solution is achieved not through any process of selection but by a deliberate intensification of the questioning itself until a breakthrough is reached. Together with faith and courage, such questioning is considered to be one of the most important mental attitudes developed through the *hwadu* practice.

MIND (K. *sim;* C. *xin;* Skt. *citta*). This key term has two distinct meanings. It is sometimes used in the normal conventional sense and thus simply refers to the cognitive faculty of man—perception, thought, or feeling—as distinct from the body. More often, though, it denotes an underlying spiritual reality that dwells at the very heart of one's being but is obscured from consciousness by the perceptions, thoughts, and feelings that are habitually focused on external objects and material concerns. This spiritual reality is also referred to by such terms as one mind, Buddha nature, true nature, and original face. To awaken to the presence of this reality is the aim of Zen meditation. In some translations the two meanings of this term are indicated by spelling the former in the lower case and by spelling the latter with a capital "M," as mind/Mind. Such a typographical distinction has not been made in this book. Not only does this spelling introduce a somewhat artificial distinction that is absent in the original language, but in many instances betrays the subtle ambiguity of certain passages which do not admit of such a hard-and-fast distinction.

BUDDHA.   There are three ways in which this word is used in this book. Often it refers to the historical Buddha, Sakyamuni, who lived and taught in India some two and a half thousand years ago. It also can be used to denote any person who has realized the enlightenment or awakening that was gained by Sakyamuni and that made him a Buddha, an awakened one. Lastly, it sometimes refers to the Buddha nature inherent within every living being, the true spiritual reality of each person; it is through an awakening to this reality that one becomes a Buddha.

The Essential Teachings are divided into four major sections. The first section, "Instructions for Meditation," outlines the practice of *hwadu* meditation as it was taught by Master Kusan. Having explained the method of taking a *hwadu* as an object of contemplation, he proceeds to describe the different stages one passes through as the practice develops. The section is concluded with a presentation of the ten diseases, that is, ten principal obstacles that hinder *hwadu* meditation.

The second section, "Discourses from a Winter Retreat," contains eight formal and two informal lectures given during the three-month winter meditation season at Songgwang Sa in 1981–82. The duration of such a retreat is measured according to the lunar calendar. The winter retreat traditionally begins at the full moon of the tenth lunar month and finishes at the full moon of the first lunar month. Thus, seven of the formal lectures were delivered at fortnightly intervals at the times of the full moon and the new moon during this period. One was given in commemoration of the Buddha's enlightenment, which, in East Asia, is celebrated on the eighth day of the twelfth lunar month. The informal talks were given privately, upon request, to the monks in the meditation hall that winter.

Much of the third section, "Advice and Encouragement,"

has been adapted from passages contained in Master Kusan's privately printed collection of teachings, *Nine Mountains*. The remaining material has been drawn from various discourses, informal talks, and dialogues that have taken place over the last few years.

The fourth section, "The Ten Oxherding Pictures," consists of ten verses composed in the Korean three-line *sijo* style. Written in vernacular Korean as opposed to classical Chinese, the verses draw upon some of the imagery found in the traditional verses of the Song-dynasty Chinese master Gaoan Shiyuan as well as Master Kusan's own personal understanding of the pictures.[6] The verses are accompanied by an oral commentary given to the monks attending the winter meditation retreat at Songgwang Sa in 1972–73.

ESSENTIAL TEACHINGS
OF THE STONE LION

At the crossroad is a stone lion. Without saying a word he informs those who pass by of the way. He welcomes the people who come and he bids farewell to those who are leaving. In complete silence he is delivering an endless Dharma discourse.[7]

So what Dharma does he preach?

> In the middle of the night as the sun rises
> The lion emerges from his cave and roars:
> The blind see and the deaf hear clearly.
> Do you understand this?

CHAPTER FIVE

Instructions for Meditation

> *Winding back and forth*
> *Among green trees*
> *The golden shuttle*
> *Of the oriole*
> *Weaves silk*
> *The color of spring.*
> *A monk sits*
> *Dozing . . .*
> *Even the stones smile.*

HWADU MEDITATION

A human being is composed of a body and a mind. A body without a mind is just a dead corpse. A mind without a body is just pure spirit. Someone who, although endowed with both a body and a mind, only knows the body but not the mind is called a sentient being. In general, a sentient being is understood as any being possessing conscious life. Birds flying in the sky, animals walking on the ground, fish swimming in the water, as well as the tiniest organisms, are all sentient beings.

Human beings are said to be superior to all other creatures. But how can a human being be considered superior if he knows his body but is ignorant of the nature of his mind? One who knows the body but not the mind is an incomplete person. However, if a human being searches for the mind and awakens to it, he will realize completeness: for at that time he will know both the body and the mind.

Such an awakened person is regarded as a Buddha, a master of all things, and a noble human being. He is one who has transcended the commonplace. The word "Buddha" means "the awakened one." Thus, if you are awakened, you will be a Buddha. But if the mind of a Buddha is obscured, he will be a sentient being. Upon awakening, this world becomes a Pure Land. But as long as you are only concerned with the body and enslaved by the environment, this world will remain as a defiled realm.

The purpose of practicing Zen meditation is to awaken to the mind. Such practice does not involve just sitting quietly and trying to calm and pacify the mind. Nor does it entail contemplating the breath. Instead it involves direct inquiry into a *hwadu*. An example of a *hwadu* would be a question such as "What is this?" or "What is this mind?"[8] What you are searching for can be called by many different names: mind, spirit, soul, true nature, and so forth. But such designations are merely labels. You should put aside all of these names and reflect on the fact that the true master of the body is more than just the label "mind." The master of the body is not the Buddha, for it is not yet awakened. Nor is it anything material, because it cannot be physically given away or received. Nor is it simply empty space, for empty space cannot pose questions or have knowledge of good and evil.

Hence there is a master who rules this body who is neither the label "mind," the Buddha, a material thing nor empty space. Having negated these four possibilities, a question will arise as to what this master really is. If you continue inquiring in this way, the questioning will become more intense. Finally, when the mass of questioning enlarges to a critical point, it will suddenly burst. The entire universe will be shattered and only your original nature will appear before you. In this way you will awaken.

It is most important to continuously investigate the *hwadu* with unswerving determination. At the beginning, you might feel as though you are trying to lift a heavy bucket full of water with a weak arm. Even so, you should never relax your effort. Instead, no matter what you are doing, be solely concerned with nothing but the *hwadu*. If a clock were unreliable and kept stopping, any sensible person would either have it repaired or get rid of it. Similarly, when practicing meditation, you must exert continuous effort and not allow yourself to be lazy.

In Zen meditation, the key factor is to maintain a constant sense of questioning. So, having taken hold of the *hwadu* "What is this?", try to always sustain the questioning: "*What* is seeing?" "*What* is hearing?" "*What* is moving these hands and feet?" and so on. Before the initial sense of questioning fades, it is important to give rise to the question again. In this way, the process of questioning can continue uninterrupted with each new question overlapping the previous one. In addition you should try to make this overlapping smooth and regular. But this does not mean that you should just mechanically repeat the question as though it were a mantra. It is useless to just say to yourself day and night, "What is this?" "What is this?" The key is to sustain the sense of questioning, not the repetition of the words. Once this inquiry gets underway there will be no room for boredom. If the mind remains quiet, the *hwadu* will not be forgotten, and the sense of questioning will continue unbroken. In this way, awakening will be easy.

While meditating, both wisdom and concentration need to be cultivated in unison. If there is wisdom without concentration, then mistaken views will increase. And if there is concentration without wisdom, then ignorance will grow. When inquiring single-pointedly into the *hwadu* "What is this?" the vividness of the *hwadu* becomes wisdom and the cessation of distracted thoughts becomes concentration.

Meditation can be compared to a battle between wandering thoughts and dullness of mind on the one side and the *hwadu* on the other. The stronger the *hwadu* becomes, the weaker will become wandering thoughts and dullness.

You are not the first and you will not be the last to tread this path. So do not become discouraged if you find the practice difficult at times. All the previous patriarchs of old as well as the contemporary masters have experienced hardships along this way. Moreover, it is not always the most virtuous or intelligent person who makes the swiftest progress. Sometimes the opposite is true. There are many cases of troublesome and ill-behaved people who, upon turning their attention inward to the practice of meditation, have quickly experienced a breakthrough. So do not feel defeated even before you have really begun.

An ancient master once said that with the passing of the days you will see your thoughts becoming identical with the *hwadu,* and the *hwadu* becoming identical with your thoughts. This is quite true. In the final analysis, the practice of Zen can be said to be both the easiest as well as the most difficult thing to do. However, do not thereby deceive yourself into thinking that it will be either very simple or extremely hard. Every morning just resolve to be awakened before evening. Strengthen this commitment daily until it is as inexhaustible as the sands along the river Ganges.

There is no one who can undertake this task for you. The student's hunger can never be satisfied by his teacher's eating a meal for him. It is like competing in a marathon. The winner will only be the person who is either the fittest or the most determined. It is solely up to the individual to win the race. Likewise, to achieve the aim of your practice, do not be distracted by things that are not related to this task. For the time being, just let everything else remain as it is and put it out of your mind. Only when you are awakened will you be able to truly benefit others.

Be careful never to disregard the moral precepts that

act as the basis for your practice of meditation. Furthermore, do not try and look deliberately withdrawn or abstracted. It is quite possible to pursue your practice of Zen without others being aware of what you are doing. However, when your absorption in the *hwadu* becomes particularly intense, your attention to external matters may diminish. This might result in your looking rather out of touch with everyday concerns. At this time the *hwadu* is said to be ripening and the mind starts to become sharper and more single-pointed, like a fine sword. It is vital at this point to pursue your practice with the intensity of an attacking soldier. You must become totally involved with the *hwadu* to the exclusion of everything else.

If you can make your body and mind become identical with the *hwadu,* then in the end ignorance will naturally shatter. You will fall into a state of complete unknowing, perplexity, and questioning. Those who have done much study will even come to forget what they had previously-learned. But this is not a final or lasting state. When you have reached this point you must still proceed further to the stage where although you have ears, you do not know how to hear; although you have eyes, you do not know how to see; and although you have a tongue, you do not know how to speak. To reach the place where mountains are not mountains and rivers are not rivers may entail several years of hard practice. Therefore, it is necessary to cast aside all other concerns and train yourself to focus the entirety of your attention on the tasteless *hwadu* alone.

By practicing diligently in this manner, you will finally awaken. Then you can seize the Buddhas and the patriarchs themselves and defeat them. At that time mountains will again be mountains, rivers will again be rivers, the earth will be the earth and the sky will be the sky. When you experience things in such a way, then you should proceed to a qualified teacher to receive confirmation of your understanding.[9]

STAGES OF MEDITATION

When people discuss the practice of meditation, they often refer to a person having either a superior, intermediate, or inferior capacity for this task. However, these capacities are not inborn qualities. For once a strong motivation has been generated, then a person is immediately endowed with a superior capacity. Nevertheless, there are different levels of motivation. Some people may leave the care of their parents and relatives and become monks or nuns with the sincere motivation to realize Buddhahood. But after practicing for a while they discover that the aim of meditation is not achieved as easily as cooling hot porridge by pouring cold water on it. Such persons may become disheartened when their practice does not proceed as smoothly as they had expected. However, a person of superior capacity is able to completely cut off the mind of discrimination as soon as he is told to do so. But for those who are unable to do this, much hardship, effort, and total determination are needed before they can achieve this state.

Your practice should always be guided by wisdom. An ancient master once said, "A wise meditator is like a cook who skillfully prepares rice for food, while a foolish meditator is like a cook who prepares sand to eat." Now, would you ever succeed in making rice by cooking grains of sand? So let us consider how to pursue our practice in a wise manner.

Most people who meditate on a *hwadu* intend at the outset to keep a firm hold on it. But usually, after a very short while, their *hwadu* disappears and they just lose themselves in delusive thoughts. If someone persists with such a practice, when will he ever awaken? Others, after a few initial attempts to hold on to the *hwadu,* find that it does not appear to them spontaneously. So they just sit still without doing anything at all. Such people then ask me, "What do you claim there to be? Surely there is just nothing."

The problem here is that although they tried to hold on to the *hwadu*, they found nothing that they could take firm hold of. Thus they conclude that there is nothing at all. But such conclusions are only reached intellectually. Indeed, as long as you continue just to scheme and conceptualize with the intellect, you will find nothing to take firm hold of. But to then proclaim that in reality there is just nothing is mere foolishness.

When the Buddha, after practicing in hills and forests for six years, finally saw a bright star and thereupon awakened, his awakening was not merely due to seeing the star. In fact it was due to his beholding a far greater brilliance. When the ancient masters gave a single-word answer to the questions of their disciples, they always had a definite reason for doing so. And when Bodhidharma talked of pointing directly to the mind of man, seeing into his original nature and thereby realizing Buddhahood, he also had a good reason for doing so. If there was in reality just nothingness, why would they have said such things? It was not just for the sake of saying something. The Buddha as well as the ancient masters and Bodhidharma all had a definite reason for saying what they did. So when an inexperienced meditator declares, "Since there is just nothing, then what are you looking for?" he is speaking meaninglessly. Moreover, such words slander the Buddhas and the patriarchs through contradicting what they said.

It is essential to take a firm hold of the *hwadu* and to continuously advance in your practice. This is the same whether you are investigating "What is this?" "No!" or "the cypress in the courtyard."[10] Initially you do not understand at all what is meant by these questions. Therefore, in order to fully understand their meaning, you must seize hold of the *hwadu* and penetrate deeply into it with incessant questioning. It is really very simple: you do not understand what is meant, thus it is necessary to find out through constant questioning. If you did understand, then, of course, there would be no need for any such questioning. The greatest disease that can affect someone who is meditating on a *hwadu* is the absence of any questioning. It is quite meaningless to simply repeat the *hwadu* mechanically in your mind without this sense of questioning.

When you first try to meditate, you may find that no matter how strong your resolve is to firmly hold the *hwadu*, the mind is constantly besieged by wandering thoughts, and it seems impossible to progress in the practice. So what should be done to correct this problem? At such times you must completely forget about what has happened in the past. For what benefit is there in continuing to think about things that have already ceased? Likewise, you should desist from speculating about what might happen in the future. For since it will be determined by various conditions, what can your present thoughts do to influence the course of future events? Your sole function during a meditation session is to sit on the meditation cushion, investigate your *hwadu*, and awaken to its meaning. Other than this there is nothing to do. So why do you needlessly waste this precious time by entertaining thoughts about what has been and what might be? However, as soon as you manage to cut off all thoughts of the past and future you will experience a state of emptiness. This occurs because at that moment both before and after are severed. If you cannot reach this state because of an inability to control your thoughts about the past and future, then you cannot be considered a true practitioner. Remember: your sole responsibility is to awaken through inquiring into the *hwadu*.

Once before and after have been severed, you enter a state of emptiness. Now at this time there is a danger that you might easily slip into a state of just observing the emptiness. In such a condition you are neither disturbed by sleepiness nor wandering thoughts, but in addition the *hwadu* is also absent. If you just observe the emptiness in this way, you will become a spineless insect. Thus, it is a mistake to merely observe the emptiness. Moreover, you should not even allow the thought to arise that you are not observing it. Likewise, try to discard even the idea that you should not allow such a thought of non-observing to arise. And finally, you should let go of that idea as well. You will then reach a point where all mental content is relinquished. At that time, since all circumstances are absent, if you take hold of the *hwadu,* it will appear with extreme vividness and clarity. By concentrating on the *hwadu* in this fashion for a period of a few days, a state of quiescence and vividness will begin to clearly emerge. At this time there is the danger of easily succumbing to the misconception that you have awakened. However, this is not an experience of awakening. It is merely a perception of the luminous nature of consciousness.

If, at such a time, you become distracted by circumstances, what is appearing to you will fade and finally become covered up. Therefore, make a great effort not to be distracted and instead continue to hold firmly on to the *hwadu.* By proceeding in this way what is appearing will become even brighter and after a short while you will reach a state in which you cannot move an inch in any direction. Even if you wanted to, you could not go forward, nor backward, nor to the right, nor to the left. Throughout, the *hwadu* remains clear, but you are simply unable to do anything. Moreover, although such a state has been reached, do not allow even the tiniest thought of having realized anything to occur. Such thoughts are a disease of the mind. Instead, in utmost earnestness, hold firmly to the *hwadu* and continue with the meditation. With such efforts you will find that even without consciously raising the *hwadu,* it will be present of its own accord. And without consciously thinking of the *hwadu,* the thought of it will always be there. At this time, when you sit, the *hwadu* sits; when you stand, the *hwadu* stands; and when you lie down, the *hwadu* lies down. When this occurs, you can truly say that the *hwadu* is present everywhere and that the practice is progressing well. Nevertheless, you must continue to persevere diligently, for there is still the danger of regressing.

Upon reaching such a state it is important to consult a wise teacher about how to proceed further with the practice. Because, on the one hand, it is easy to mistake such experiences for an awakening, and, on the other, you simply may be at a loss as to what should next be done. Now, a wise teacher in this case is one who is able to clearly show the way ahead so that your practice can progress. However, there are some teachers who, through a lack of understanding, will tell you to select another *hwadu* at this point. But this is not good advice and such persons are unwise teachers. At this time, that which stands between yourself and awakening is as thin as a single sheet of white paper. It is the responsibility of a good teacher to show as clearly as he can the correct method to break through it.

At this time you need to proceed with the same keen determination and enthusiasm as a beginner. Now the moment has come to raise the final resolve. At the outset of the practice your resolve can be compared to soaking the straw with which to make sandals in water. Now, as the practice approaches its goal, your final resolve must be similar to that of someone who has to slash through an impossible knot with a single stroke of his sword. All other concerns must be indiscriminately cast aside. If you are to die, then you will die; if you are to live, then you will live. Through developing such determination, the task can now be completed within one week. Thus, realizing this to be a very critical moment, you should prepare yourself with all intensity for one more bout. This then is the final resolve.

You might wonder why it does not matter whether meditators live or die at this point. The reason is that even should they die while practicing in this way, their spirits will proceed to a place of meditation, that is to say, the place where all the Buddhas are residing. Because they have entered the state of quiescence and vividness where their *hwadu* appear with extreme clarity, upon dying they will give no thought at all to the body and instead naturally proceed to such a place of meditation. Therefore, even if they die, they are certain to attain the goal. And if they live, they will gain the certainty of an awakening; for now they are standing right before the door of enlightenment. It is as though merely a sheet of white paper were barring their way. A single abrupt word from a wise teacher will suffice for them to burst through right then and there.

THE TEN DISEASES

The ten diseases are ten errors that need to be avoided when meditating on a *hwadu*. They were originally compiled by the Chinese master Dahui, and are also listed in the works of the Korean master Chinul. They are specifically intended for those working on the *hwadu* "No!" This *hwadu* came about in the following way. In Tang dynasty China there was once a well-known Zen master called Zhaozhou. One day a monk approached him and asked whether a dog possessed the Buddha-nature or not. To this question Zhaozhou replied, "No!" (C. *wu*; J. *mu*). However, the Buddha clearly stated that every sentient being is endowed with the Buddha-nature. Why, then, did Zhaozhou reply, to the contrary, "No!"? Prior to giving the answer, what did Zhaozhou have in mind that prompted him to say "No!"? To pursue such inquiry is what is meant by meditating on the *hwadu* "No!" Nevertheless, the following advice is equally pertinent to all forms of *hwadu* practice.

1. *Do not entertain thoughts of "is" or "is not," "has" or "has not."* While contemplating "No!" some people start forming opinions about the nature of "is," "is not," and so

forth. They speculate as to whether "is not" proceeds from "is," or if "is" originates from "is not." When practicing this meditation, do not entertain any such discursive thoughts. Just keep the *hwadu* firmly in mind.

2. *Do not think that Zhaozhou said "No!" because in reality there is just nothing.* When Zhaozhou uttered "No!" it was his way of expressing the truth. Thus "No!" is not just a negation implying nothingness. Nowadays, if the mind does not appear to people quickly and they are unable to awaken to it, they conclude that actually there is no mind, and so it was for this reason that Zhaozhou said "No!" At other times they may reach a state in their meditation where everything is quiet and still. This may also give rise to the idea that in reality nothing at all exists and for this reason Zhaozhou replied "No!" However, all such speculations are a disease of the mind.

3. *Do not resort to principles or theories.* Nowadays it is common for people to inquire about the nature of truth. However, instead of trying to directly awaken to it, they try to describe it in terms of certain principles and theories, such as that of fate, for example. There are many people who thus reason and speculate about what truth is by merely reducing it to this or that principle, and then speak as though they had actually awakened to it. Such understanding is not the result of awakening but of mere intellectual speculation: it is just a disease of the mind.

4. *Do not try to resolve the* hwadu *by making it an object of intellectual inquiry.* One will never succeed in gaining true understanding through thinking about the *hwadu* intellectually or through just studying the words of the Buddhas and patriarchs. The purpose of the Buddha dharma is to awaken, not to accumulate intellectual knowledge.

5. *When the master raises his eyebrows or blinks his eyes, do not take such things for indications about the meaning of Dharma.* It is mistaken to try and answer a question such as "What is the mind?" by merely raising your eyebrows or blinking your eyes. It is likewise mistaken to raise your fist as an expression of the mind or the truth.

6. *Do not regard the skillful use of words as a means to express the truth.* However gifted you may be in language and in the art of speaking, it is a mistake to think that such means can reveal truth itself. All that they are capable of doing is to vocally express one's intentions.

7. *Do not confuse a state of vacuity and ease for realization of the truth.* As you continue in your practice you may reach a point where there is no "I," no universe, no delusive thoughts, and no *hwadu.* In such a state you find it easy and comfortable to just remain still without doing anything. However, to remain still and quiet without the *hwadu* is merely a state of mental dullness. It is not true practice. The result of practicing in such a way is to be reborn as a spineless insect.

8. *Do not take the place where you become aware of sense-objects to be the mind.* You should not consider the mind to be that which reflects upon visual forms, sounds, tastes, and tactile sensations. Many people think that the mind is simply that which reflects upon what is seen and heard and is able to distinguish between good, bad, and so forth. Thus they regard the sixth sense, the intellect, to be the mind. But such views are just delusive thinking. Before seeing, before feeling, and before thinking: what is the mind? This alone is what you have to search for and awaken to.

9. *Do not just rely upon words quoted from the teachings.* It is of no help to construct your own interpretation of the

Buddha's sutras or the sayings of the patriarchs. Such activities are just a deluded way of thinking. However, once you awaken to the original mind, what was previously just deluded thinking will be transformed into wisdom. After you have awakened, then you will naturally speak the words of the Buddhas and patriarchs.

Sometimes learned teachers spend their time writing books. In these texts they discuss such topics as the dialogues between monks and great masters. They then refer to their work as discourses on Dharma. There are many nowadays who write such books. But of what real benefit is such work to their fundamental task? There is not really much benefit. To search through books for information and to then proclaim it yourself is like eating the leftovers of someone else's meal. To consider this alone as your practice is like going to the beach and trying to count all the grains of sand there.

You might object that these instructions too are words in a book and therefore should be discarded. But paying attention to what is said here can be very helpful in checking your own meditation practice. From time to time it is necessary to turn your attention back on the practice itself to make sure that you have not contracted any one of these ten diseases.

10. *Do not just remain in a deluded state waiting for enlightenment to happen.* This means that you will get nowhere by just keeping the *hwadu* in mind devoid of any questioning. In addition, it points out the mistaken attitude of thinking that if you stay in a monastery long enough, you will eventually realize enlightenment.

CHAPTER SIX

Discourses From a Winter Retreat

I made friends with the white clouds
    and grey storks
Who gently reply to the fresh wind
    and the bright moon.
Unaffected by the passage of time
I remain bright and quiet while I sit.
A bowl of porridge,
A plate of wild greens,
And a cup of tea:
I smile.

FIRST LECTURE

I venture to ask the assembly: all of you who are endowed with a pure, undefiled original nature—have you completely awakened to it or not? If by chance you have penetrated the profound meaning of the patriarchs, then say something! You may know the unchanging nature by seeing bamboos and pines in the snow. Do you understand?

> With the cessation of defilements, there is
>   no high or low place.
> The pure original face cannot be assailed.
> In ice, flames appear; the bright light is
>   all-pervasive.

The subtle Dharma, limitless as the sands
along the Ganges, adorns the entire world.

Although many rivers converge in the sea, in the end their
taste is one and the flow of their waters comes to an end.
Likewise, defilements and false thinking endlessly flow
from the conditioned mind. Due to this we suffer beneath
the wheel of birth and death. But when the mind from
which defilements and false thinking flow is completely
cut off, the high and the low disappear. Common and accomplished beings vanish. Originally, all is equal. Therefore, the pure original face cannot be assailed. (*The master
strikes his staff on the base of his seat and then holds it before
the assembly.*) The pure original nature that is able to hear
this sound and see this staff cannot be assailed. It does not
undergo the suffering of birth and death. It is not stained
by defilements.

All of you who came to this monastery: what are you
doing? Are you eagerly seeking fame and wealth? Are
you seeking glory? Are you just looking for comfort? Did
you come to the temple to live free from cares because
life in the world is too difficult? Are you eagerly seeking
scholastic learning? Are you eagerly seeking cleverness?
You should not be here for any of these reasons.

All the affairs of the world are just like dreams. With a
single stroke of a knife completely sever all concerns! Only
search for awakening. Not only must you discard all worldly fame, wealth, glory, comfort, learning, and cleverness,
but the Buddhas as well. You must finish with it all.

An ancient master once said, "The bright light of the
mind has never darkened. From ages past to the present
it has been the brilliant Way. When entering this door,
discard intellectual knowledge." This bright spiritual light,
which is able to hear this sound and see this staff, has not
darkened even once. Not once has it become a sentient
being. Not once has it become a Buddha. For this reason,

it is the Way that is eternally radiant. Therefore, when entering this door, discard intellectual knowledge. After practicing for a while, you may come to think that you know something. Then you start conceptualizing. For example, if you have been meditating on "No!" you may think, "That which says 'No!'—is that not it?" Those working on "What is this?" may think, "That which says 'What is this?'—is that not it?" This approach is wrong. Therefore, avoid speculative thinking.

You must possess truthfulness and sincerity in order to practice correctly. To practice simply because others are doing so is just imitation. You will never achieve anything in that way. You must truly awaken in order to be freed from the suffering of birth and death. Knowledge and conceptualization are not appropriate. When you awaken to the genuine truth, you will stand out in the world and be called a supreme being. Such a person extensively benefits both the sentient and the nonsentient and is called a master of all things. Since he brings the suffering of birth and death to an end forever, he becomes lord of the ten thousand things.

When you investigate the *hwadu* and intend to awaken to your great original nature, you must be like a hen hatching eggs. Think about how much effort the hen must exert in order to successfully hatch eggs. From dawn to dusk she constantly pecks and searches for food. Imagine how hungry she gets while sitting on the eggs all day long. If she frequently leaves to eat or drink, only half of them will hatch properly; the rest will rot. While the hen is hatching her eggs, she does not just sit quietly. She moves the eggs around with her feet in order to evenly distribute the heat. Only in this way will the chicks hatch successfully.

It is the same for somebody practicing meditation. Whether you are investigating "What is this?" "No!" or "the cypress in the courtyard" the practice will not mature if you just hold the *hwadu* motionless. If you just watch it, repeating, "What is this?" "What is this? . . ." then you would be like a hen trying to hatch her eggs without moving them. This would be foolish. You cannot awaken in this manner. You must be like the hen who moves her eggs around. When Zhaozhou said, "No!" what was his reason for saying it? You must inquire into this. Why did he say "No!"? To express himself in words already spoiled it. What was his state of mind prior to uttering, "No!"? Sitting still, merely keeping the *hwadu* in mind is not correct practice. It is just like "watching the tree, waiting for the rabbit."[11] You must diligently investigate with a mind willing to endure even the crushing of your bones. What is this? What is it like? Is it long or short? You must continually penetrate into the question with a profound sense of inquiry.

By maintaining such practice for a while, you may enter an empty state whereupon body, self, and world disappear. But the practice is not solely concerned with reaching this state. The Buddha expounded the doctrine of emptiness because of the disease of existence. But this doctrine is not the only teaching. Emptiness can also be a disease. To only remain in this state is comparable to polishing a tile with the hope of transforming it into a mirror. Thus, to simply watch emptiness is also a disease. Existence and emptiness can both be diseases.

There are some people who try to obtain wisdom through book knowledge. This is comparable to going to the seashore and trying to count all the grains of sand. Could you ever count each one of them? The true meditator, after selecting a *hwadu,* must consider it as his very life. When going, the *hwadu* goes; when coming, the *hwadu* comes; when eating, the *hwadu* eats; when sleeping, the *hwadu* sleeps. Even when going to the toilet and defecating, you must investigate earnestly, never letting the *hwadu* out of your mind, to the point where it seems that the *hwadu* itself is defecating.

At times while practicing, your head may ache and become hot. This is often due to the arising of *sanggi*.[12] You should not think that when *sanggi* occurs you should stop practicing. The arising of *sanggi* should never prevent anyone from continuing to practice. For example, my teacher Hyobong Sunim would continue to practice in spite of the fact that he had developed painful sores on his buttocks. Once when he contracted *sanggi*, he reported to his teacher Soktu Sunim that his head was so painful that he thought he would die. His teacher jokingly replied, "Very good! A meditator contracting *sanggi* is like a young woman becoming pregnant. It is a sign of a task being brought to completion." Hyobong Sunim inquired further, "Contracting *sanggi* isn't fatal, is it?" "No, it is not," answered his teacher. Thus, he decided that there was no cause for worry and resumed his practice. Within fifteen days his *sanggi* disappeared. It was the same way with me. I contracted *sanggi* during my first retreat. I was walking lopsidedly, off balance. My teeth felt like they were falling out, and my eyes were sinking into their sockets. I reflected that this is an illusory body. Since it will inevitably perish, I determined to either let it die now or bring my practice to completion. With this resolution I pursued my practice diligently and soon all the effects of *sanggi* disappeared.

A wise spiritual teacher would not suggest that someone postpone meditation and rest for a while upon contracting *sanggi*. For example, at the time of the Buddha, Ananda was once expending such great efforts in his practice that he felt his head would burst. He then started to worry about how to deal with this *sanggi* he had contracted. At that moment a god appeared in the sky and explained to him that the pain in his head was due to the transformation from a common to an accomplished being. Since it was not really a disease, he should not regard it as one and thus stop practicing. To do so would be like intending to remain a common sentient being.

Unless he has been practicing for many lives, it is inevitable that a meditator's head may ache occasionally. The sixth patriarch, Huineng, labored all day long pounding rice with a stone on his back and making fire for the whole community while still maintaining a very steady practice. For such an individual there are no insurmountable problems.

You must also be like a cat trying to catch a mouse. Observe the look of a cat that is trying to catch a mouse at the foot of a stone wall. While slinking along at the base of the wall, it keeps its eyes firmly fixed on the hole where the mouse entered. At a place far away from the hole it then sits silently in hiding. Its eyes continue to stare piercingly at the hole while waiting for the mouse to come out. At such a time even if a person, a chicken, or a dog goes near the cat, it takes no notice of their passing and continues to watch the mouse hole. If the mouse appears for even an instant, like a flash of lightning, it leaps and grabs it. If even a cat proceeds so mindfully when trying to catch a mouse, how much more so should a person pursue awakening when practicing meditation.

Furthermore, you must practice with a feeling of urgency as though you were trying to extinguish a fire burning on your head. In such a situation would you stop to ponder, "Is this heat due to fire?" or "Is it really burning or not?" Is there anybody present here who would experiment and let the fire burn for a while to see how well it burns? Under such circumstances, without thinking, you would immediately brush your hand over your head in order to get rid of the fire. You should cultivate meditation with the same sense of urgency.

To live long would be to live for a hundred years. A short life is over in the time it takes to inhale and exhale a single breath. A hundred years of life depends upon a single breath, for life stops when respiration ceases. Can you afford to wait for a hundred years when you do not know how soon death will come? You may die after having eaten a good breakfast in the morning; you may die in the afternoon after a good lunch. Some die during sleep. You may die in the midst of going here and there. No one can determine the time of death. Therefore, you must awaken before you die.

> In the Dharmadhatu of the ten directions,
> The ten thousand defilements and subtle
> functions all arise from your own mind.
> Where will you seek the Buddha's truth?
> The toad in the snow catches and swallows
> the tiger.

Look at the sea. Not only when there is wind do waves arise. Even when the sea is calm, waves are rising and falling thousands of times.

A defiled person will call this world a sea of suffering. An awakened one will call it a Buddha world. At that time, the ten thousand things will be transformed into the ten thousand subtle functions. For an enlightened person, it is simply all illuminated. For a defiled person, it is simply all defiled. All is arising from your own mind. The Buddha world arises from your own mind. Its transformation into the sea of suffering likewise arises from your own mind.

Assembly, reflect on this! I trust that your practice will progress during this winter retreat.

SECOND LECTURE

Since we have entered this meditation retreat, two weeks have gone by. Now only seventy-five days remain. Truly, where is the subtle principle?

If you awaken to the Dharma of one mind, simultaneously

you will completely penetrate the thousand kinds of concentration and the countless subtle fundamental principles. In one moment you will pierce all the one thousand seven hundred koans. Assembly gathered here, have you reached this place or not? He who has reached it, say something! What is the Dharma of one mind?

The stones are flowing, but the water is not. Because the moon is shining brightly, the area illuminated is without limit. If you have not been able to awaken to the Dharma of one word, all heedless talk and many thousands of lines of reasonings will be just like snowflakes falling on a hot furnace. Therefore, what should we actually do? Assembly gathered here, what will you do?

The Dharma of the awakened mind is the principal gateway through which the Buddhas of the three times, the patriarchs, the bodhisattvas in the ten directions, the spiritual advisors of this present age, and all sentient beings are coming and going. It does not make any difference whether you are a sentient being or a spiritual advisor. All alike are coming and going through this door.

If you awaken to this door, you are called a Buddha. If you are deluded about it, you are called a sentient being. This door itself is bright, clear, empty, and profound. Yet even though it is empty, in the midst of this emptiness, it is also profound. Originally, it is undifferentiated. Between the Buddhas, the patriarchs, the bodhisattvas, the spiritual advisors, and all sentient beings there is actually no distinction. However, if this door becomes obscured, you will transmigrate endlessly throughout the suffering ocean of birth and death. Yet if you awaken to it, the sublime Dharmadhatu will appear brilliantly clear before your eyes. In one of his lectures, Master Linji said, "When one word is brilliantly clear, millions of worlds are transcended."

The sufferings of transmigrating within the ocean of birth and death, as well as the happiness of the sublime

Dharmadhatu appearing brilliantly clear before your eyes, do not come from outside. They are also not given to us by anyone else. You do not have to endure sufferings because someone else gave them to you. Neither does somebody else grant you happiness. They are created and experienced by yourself alone. You have to endure sufferings because you created them yourself. Likewise, you experience happiness because you have created it yourself.

During the twenty-four hours of the day, in all of the four positions, when you are coming, the *hwadu* should be coming; and when you are going, the *hwadu* should also be going. You should investigate earnestly, carefully, and in detail. I always carefully observe meditators when they are walking here and there. How many hold the *hwadu* firmly? Usually, when they are coming and going or eating, they completely forget about the *hwadu* and just act blindly according to circumstances. With such practice, it is hard to say when such people will ever awaken. You must pay a great deal of attention to this point.

You should take great awakening as your aim and model and never let the mind be at ease. If you act without caring to raise the *hwadu,* mind and body will surely be at ease. But this is just like water flowing away. Indeed, the lives of sentient beings flow away like this. Now, having taken up the practice of "ten thousand actions," you should endure what is difficult to endure and do what is difficult to do. This is known as "austerity," for the very reason that it involves undergoing what is difficult. The Buddhas and the patriarchs did not realize Buddhahood easily. They realized it through great effort and much hardship. They exerted themselves with such great effort because the sufferings of birth and death are so terrifying. Therefore, even though you want to sleep more, you should sleep less. Even though you want to eat more, you should eat less. Even though you want to talk a lot, you should try to talk less. Even though you want to see many things, you should see less.

Your body will definitely feel restrained by acting in such a way. This is indeed a practice of austerity. However, none of the Buddhas and the patriarchs would have awakened had they not trained themselves in this manner.

Being bound by circumstances originates from the mind's own bondage. Likewise, liberation from the suffering of birth and death ensues from the mind's being liberated from them. This is the Dharma of one mind. Everything there is proceeds from this one mind. Access to the doors of both liberation and bondage lies' in your own hands. It is not dependent upon anyone else. It is not dependent upon the Buddhas nor the patriarchs nor the spiritual advisors. It is solely in your own hands.

> All the mountains, all the rivers—such a beau-
>   tiful landscape!
> During endless aeons, in each life, this world has
>   appeared—no amount of praise could be enough.
> It is not the product of anyone's strength;
> Every single aspect of it arises from your own mind.

Last autumn the maple trees were a brilliant red; the chrysanthemums, fragrant; the mountains and rivers, a magnificent sight. When we see all these beautiful things, we all know how to be happy. During endless aeons, in every life, we have been praising such things. It is not only this one time that we have praised them. When the moon is bright and the wind blows, some say that the moon is shining brightly and a refreshing wind is blowing. However, others say that the moon looks bleak and the wind is dreary. In reality, do you think that the moon is shining brightly to some and bleakly to others? This is not the case. These are circumstantial impressions arising from their own minds.

In brief, to awaken to the mind should be your fundamental goal.

THIRD LECTURE

Since the subtle wisdom of complete enlightenment has been present even before the creation of the Earth, it has never been lost. Why do you say that you are looking for it again? From long ago until now, it has been unimpeded and has been shining brightly and tranquilly. Assembly gathered here today, have you completely awakened to it or not? If there is a monk endowed with the Dharma eye, let him say something! In reality, what is this subtle wisdom of complete enlightenment? *Hak!*

When a stone tiger gives birth to a lion cub and a wooden woman becomes pregnant, only then will you understand.

> With a wooden staff one strikes
> Mount Sumeru.
> Everything is contained in the midst of
> a sound that echoes like thunder.
> Who can say that he has secretly buried
> a precious gem deep in the ground?
> The piercing wisdom is like an awl in a bag.

This stanza refers to a well-known story in China that concerned a certain Mr. Hwa. This man once obtained a precious gem that was able to emit light at night, a fresh breeze in summer, and a warm wind in winter. Of course he tried to hide this gem from others and thus used to bury it deep in the ground. But however deep he hid it, the authorities always found it and took it away from him. Likewise, when someone awakens, he is unable to hide his wisdom. Little by little, it will become apparent. Furthermore, however carefully you put an awl inside a bag, it is sure to pierce it and extrude. Likewise, if you are practicing meditation, others will be able to judge this by observing your outer appearance. Even if you try, you will not be able to deceive them.

Let me introduce you to a few words from a lecture of Master Zongjing. He once said, "All sentient beings are covered by the six dusts." This means that they are covered by the six kinds of thieves that come from the outside. In addition, "they are enmeshed in the five aggregates. Thus, they are coming and going along the path of birth and death." However, "their original nature is never obscured." Therefore, "if a poor woman were in possession of a treasure, she would bury it so deeply that no one would be able to dig it up and take it away." But even if someone were to take it away, it would still remain the same; and if the poor woman kept it in her possession, it would also remain the same. This treasure will always stay just as it is. Moreover, "even though a diamond is extracted from very deep within the earth, it cannot be destroyed." You should bear this in mind. The wisdom of your original nature is always clear and bright. It never changes. On becoming a Buddha, that wisdom is present. On becoming an animal, that wisdom is present. Wherever you go within the six realms of the suffering ocean of existence, that wisdom appears just as it is, without ever changing. But why do you not realize this? Because you are covered by the six dusts and enmeshed in the five aggregates. With the beak of wisdom, break through the skin of ignorance that covers you! When you finally break through the skin of ignorance with the inquiring beak of wisdom, you will then be freed from the three worlds and thus liberated from the ocean of suffering. Being without any further hindrances or restrictions, the mind will now experience complete equanimity. It will shine forth clearly and brightly, leaving you with no more doubts. At such a time what could possibly be in opposition to the mind or comparable to it?

This year a good assembly of monks has gathered here in the monastery and is indeed making sincere efforts to practice meditation. Assembly, within this year you must really break through the skin of ignorance! But this is not done easily and quickly. You must first give rise to the greatest possible faith and determination. You must be prepared to die. Often you practice just because others are doing so, with no urgency at all. You think that it is as easy as cooling hot porridge by simply pouring a little cold water over it. Your meditation will never progress if you practice in such a way. It cannot be accomplished as easily as that. Now, you must try to simply cast your body aside and consider it just like a stone cast to the roadside. Such a stone would be thrown aside because of its uselessness. Its size and shape serve no purpose at all. Whether winds blow or rains fall, that stone simply remains as it is. When covered with snow and ice, it remains unchanged. Even if someone walks on it, it still remains as it is. Impassively, the stone never changes; it simply remains as it is: a stone cast aside. Therefore, when you practice meditation, without speculating or conceptualizing, cast your body aside!

> When the mind of a sentient being appears
>   clear and bright, he is called a Buddha.
> When the mind of a Buddha is obscured,
>   he is called a sentient being.
> In its own nature the one mind is always
>   unchanging.
> When it appears distinctly and clearly, it is
>   called the "Great Mirror Wisdom."

FOURTH LECTURE

Today is the last day of the lunar month. The new moon is so bright that its light pervades the entire Dharmadhatu. Long ago Master Nanquan once took his assembly of monks to look at the moon. So is this moon I am talking of the same as or different from the moon that Master Nanquan gazed at? Those of you monks who are endowed with the Dharma eye, say something!

Even though you may claim to have awakened, I would still give you thirty blows. How many more would those who have not awakened receive?

> Casting a fishing line of a thousand feet
>   into the ocean of space,
> The clouds disperse, the waves settle,
>   and the coral grows.
> The fish and the dragons sleep deeply and
>   do not move.
> Load the ship full with the moon, pull
>   the oar and depart.

Assembly of monks, it is true that these days you are exerting much effort in your practice of meditation. However, I would like to add a few words for your benefit. Of the ninety days of this winter retreat, already half have passed, for today we have reached the midpoint of the meditation season, and only forty-five days are now left. Every day time flows on urgently like water. Even though it may seem that there are certain enjoyments in daily life, actually we are just like fish in a pool whose water is constantly being drained away. When all the water has gone, the fish will surely die, won't they? Likewise, not only you monks gathered here but all sentient beings are traveling the path that only leads to death. As each day passes, your life span decreases by one day. And as each hour passes, it decreases by one hour. Just listen to this clock. With every tick the second hand moves, pauses, and moves on again. This itself can immediately be taken as a Dharma lecture of the Buddha. Therefore, the *mara* of transiency is propelling us toward death every moment. If you do not realize the truth of the unborn, then when the time of death suddenly arrives, you will find yourself moaning in illness. Even though nobody wants to die, every one of us will inevitably perish. Is there anyone here among you whose body is not a potential corpse? If there is, then speak out! Furthermore, should we live solely for the benefit of this potential corpse? Or would it be better to live in order to awaken to the truth of the unborn? When you are finally moaning in illness, then you may have regrets at not having diligently practiced while alive. But at that time such regrets will be in vain. Therefore, why do you not practice now? Why do you just continue to play around?

The mind is just like the moon rising behind a mass of clouds. It seems dim because its brightness, like the brightness of the moon, is obscured and cannot shine forth. However, if the mind is purified, a Buddha will appear. People will say that from the day you awakened a Buddha appeared in the world anew. But in reality no Buddha ever came. Originally the mind is there, bright and illuminating. It does not become bright for the first time only when you awaken. When the mind is sullied, an ordinary man appears. Then people say that a Buddha has departed and that the world has become that of sentient beings. But in reality a Buddha never departed. Therefore, a Buddha does not appear upon purification of the mind and likewise does not depart when the mind becomes sullied. Be careful not to fall into either of these two extremes.

Keep your *hwadu* bright and do not let it darken. Everything else can be left aside, but the *hwadu* should be considered as your own life. You must try to investigate it like an old mouse entering a cow horn. In some countries, when people want to catch a mouse, they will put some fragrant oil in the pointed end of a horn and place it near the mouse's hole. The mouse is attracted by the smell and, once it thinks it is safe, crawls into the horn. It gets nearer and nearer the oil until finally its body gets stuck in the pointed end and it is unable to withdraw. In order to taste the oil the foolish mouse has no fear of death and without any hesitation crawls right to the end of the horn. When even a mouse can be as brave as this in order to get what it desires, shouldn't human beings put forth a similar determination of mind in order to resolve the great matter of birth and death and to realize the great truth of the universe? Shouldn't human beings cease to be preoccupied with this body and one time exert themselves in order to awaken?

You should practice with the same urgency as a person with a parched throat thinking of water. When you are very thirsty during a long walk in the mountains, for example, you may feel that you are about to choke from thirst and die unless you can soon drink some water. At such a time, you only think of water. Now if you were to dig a well to find some, you would probably die before being able to reach any source of water. Therefore, you look earnestly all around you for water until you find some. In order to resolve the great matter of birth and death you must practice with the same lack of preoccupation with the body as the mouse entering a cowhorn, and with the same urgency and earnestness as a thirsty man searching for water. If you practice like this for some time, you will reach a point where the mind has nowhere left to go. At that moment, thoughts are absent and all delusive thinking comes to a complete halt. At such a time the mass of questioning alone appears brilliantly before your eyes. Now your practice may actually seem easy. But you should be most careful, since this is a very crucial moment. You must hold on to the *hwadu* with the same degree of energy as you would have upon meeting an enemy after ten thousand years and being resolute on taking revenge. Throughout beginningless aeons you have been transmigrating through the suffering ocean of birth and death. Now, for one time, the mass of questioning is clear and awakening is very close by. It is as though it were screened off by a single sheet of white paper. Soon the moment will arrive when you can take revenge on birth and death through achieving liberation from them. In order to avenge yourself of such an enemy who has tormented you for so long, shouldn't you exert yourself to the utmost? You must be determined to pass over this crucial step. Otherwise, if you let it go by, the *hwadu* will gradually lose its vividness and it will be even harder to reach such a state again. Therefore, do not waste this opportunity!

At this time you will automatically forget to even sleep or eat. To not let this opportunity slip by requires true wisdom. So do not waste it. Be as resolute as the Buddha when he sat for seven days uninterruptedly. The Buddha left home forty-one aeons after Maitreya Buddha but because he sat beneath the bodhi tree for seven days uninterruptedly, he was the first to realize Buddhahood. In the same manner, you must practice hard and diligently, being unconcerned whether you live or die. Then, finally, a great awakening will be near.

> Having transcended all intellection and
>   perception, not even the slightest trace of
>   any hindrance will remain.
> Your oceanlike chest will extend to the limits of
>   space, the four walls will crumble,
> And the Buddhas of the three times will not be
>   seen anywhere.
> Without taking even a single step, you will
>   ascend to the lotus realm.

To transcend intellection means to no longer follow the impulses of conceptual consciousness. In addition, you must transcend all perceptions such as seeing, hearing, and mental cognition. In this way no hindrances will remain since both before and after will have been completely cut off. Then the four elements of earth, water, fire, and air contained in the body as well as the universe become void. When you undergo such experiences, it is a sign that your practice is developing well. But if you only try to reason and conceptualize intellectually while practicing, then you are merely indulging in childish games. For such an approach involves only delusive thinking. When nothing remains that can taint the mind, then the four elements disappear and reveal a vast and boundless space. At this time the pure original face will appear.

Upon awakening you become one with the Buddha and therefore cannot see the Buddha. You do not have to come or go anywhere. Right where you are is the very Buddha world. Even though you yourself are actually a Buddha living in a Buddha world, you do not realize this because your mind is obscured. Just awaken to the fact that you are a Buddha and this world will be revealed just as it is, that is, as a Buddha world. There is no gain and no loss, no Buddha and no sentient beings. All is equal. All is a Buddha world. And all sentient beings, just as they are, are all Buddhas. For this reason, the Buddha said in the Diamond Sutra, "The Dharma I preach is no Dharma. Even though I speak, nothing is being said."

LECTURE COMMEMORATING
THE BUDDHA'S ENLIGHTENMENT

As the assembly already knows, today is the anniversary of the Buddha's enlightenment. It is also the day for a ceremony, being the forty-ninth day after the death of Pak Ilgwi from the city of Kwangju.[13]

If you say that the Buddha awakened, you would be slandering him. If you say that the Buddha did not awaken, you would also be slandering him. If you say that Pak Ilgwi lived, it would be like saying that clouds formed and covered the sky. If you say that he died and departed, then it would be like saying that imaginary flowers fell at random from the sky. Do not fall into either of these two extremes! All of you monks gathered here, say something!

Hak!

Even though the mountains move, the moon does not. Everywhere is a place of enlightenment.

Actually, if you say this is easy to understand, it will be easy. If you say it is difficult to understand, then it will be difficult. The Buddha renounced the world and on the eighth day of the twelfth lunar month realized Buddhahood. It is a historical fact that he left the palace, retreated to the hills and forests, practiced for six years and finally awakened. However, if you say that the Buddha awakened anew, you would be slandering him. Why? Because he attained that which does not need to be attained. Originally he was already endowed with Buddhahood. Then why did he demonstrate the eight deeds of a fully enlightened being? His doing so was just an expedient means to lead others to liberation. Thus it is wrong to say that he either did or did not realize Buddhahood.

As for layman Pak Ilgwi, in a certain way it seems that he was born and then passed away. But in reality no birth and death took place. If he had really died then what would be the use of doing a forty-ninth-day ceremony today? It is only because there is definitely something that does not die that a memorial ceremony is being performed.

> The thousand world systems are originally
> the Dharma body.
> The eighty-four-thousand lesser actions turn
> the wheel of Dharma.
> Since birth and death are fundamentally
> empty, they permeate a single path.
> All distinctions are actually Nirvana.

The thousand world systems are originally the clear and pure Dharma body of Vairocana, the original body of

Shakyamuni, the original body of the deceased Pak Ilgwi, and the original body of those of you gathered here today. The Buddha's demonstrating the realization of Buddhahood and Pak Ilgwi's undergoing the process of birth and death are both the turning of the wheel of Dharma. In reality, even though you may realize Buddhahood, there is nothing that can be said to have been realized. And even though you die, there is nothing that can be said to have died. Therefore, to show the Dharma in all its manifoldness is to reveal Nirvana.

The lecture should formally be concluded here. However, I am afraid that the deceased may not have understood what I have said above. Therefore, I would like to add a few more words. Deceased Pak Ilgwi, listen once more to these words! (*The master lifts his staff, strikes it once on the base of his seat and holds it up to the assembly.*) You can hear this sound very clearly and you can see this staff very distinctly. What is it that knows how to hear and see clearly? Indeed, what is it? As flames spring forth from ice and snow, a stone cow is bellowing.

If, disregarding the mind, you are only concerned with the body and become entangled in external affairs, this world will be a samsaric world for you. Yet the Buddha never departed from such a world. He remains here just as he is. So if you relinquish worldly enjoyments, search for the mind, and awaken to it, this world will become a Buddha world for you. Moreover, the Buddha never came here. Both departing and coming are fundamentally empty. Birth and death are not two. The Dharma of nonduality is the very Buddha dharma itself. What is meant by nonduality? It means that fundamentally there is no coming or going, no birth or death, no being a man or a woman, no being an ordinary person or an accomplished one, and no nearness or distance. This should be understood to be the essence of the Buddha dharma.

Birth is just like the formation of clouds in the sky and

death is like their dispersal. Although a difference seems to be created by the formation and dispersal of clouds, space itself remains unaffected. Likewise, ultimate reality is also immutable. With no apparent purpose this body comes into being. We then mistake it for a self, and for a while, remain under this illusion. However, when the four physical elements of the body disintegrate, the mind alone— today that of Pak Ilgwi—appears clear and bright. This is similar to when clouds are dispersed throughout ten thousand miles and the solitary sun shines forth.

Although we go, there is no going; although we come, there is no coming. Thus, Pak Ilgwi roams freely through the worlds of the ten directions. Likewise, beings come and go as they wish, to and from the Pure Lands and the Buddha realms. At this time they are truly joyful. This body is a burden for us as it is bound by materiality. When coming, it suffers; when going, it suffers. It is limited as to where it can go. With this body we cannot go to the Pure Lands or the Buddha realms, for example. Complete freedom to come and go is only present when the mind alone appears brilliantly. What great joy to have such freedom!

> Do not say that you have no choice to live
>   long or to die early:
> The original nature being as it is, you are
>   always free to roam at will.
> Long ago as well as now, clear and pure, it
>   is very subtle.
> From the top of a shadowless tree, flowers
>   never fall.

Why has the original nature always been so clear and pure? Because even though countless aeons have passed, it has never changed, and, even though time may endlessly elapse, it will never change. Therefore, at the top of a shadowless tree, flowers are always blooming.

What is the true Dharma that each one of you is endowed with? The monk who possesses the Dharma eye, say something about this true Dharma!

Hak!

When the sun rises in the middle of the night, the midday bell is rung.

> The true wisdom of the one mind is
> my body.
> It is always clear and tranquilly appears
> before the eyes.
> Why is the cold white goose, high in
> the sky, crying?
> The snow and the moon are mutually
> bright, illuminating all human and
> heavenly realms.

True wisdom is always and everywhere clear because it is conditioned neither by past or present, nor by ordinary men or accomplished ones, nor by men or women, nor by delusion or enlightenment. In no way is it limited.

Let me introduce you to a few words of Master Zongjing. He once said, "The liberation of all the Buddhas must be sought within the workings of each sentient being's mind. It should not be sought elsewhere." This means that the subtle Nirvanic mind will only be found within the everyday functionings of the mind and nowhere else. Originally, there is no distinction between Buddhas and sentient beings. However, to use a simile, it is as though clouds were covering the blue sky. For even though the sun is present, its brightness is not visible. Yet when the clouds disperse it is seen to shine clearly. In this case it is not the sun that undergoes any change. However, the difference between brightness and darkness is as great as that between heaven and earth. There is a similar difference between Buddhas and sentient beings. When defilements completely obscure the mind, it is like when clouds are covering a valley.

Now, if you awaken to your original nature, the sun will rise behind the western mountains. Although the sun generally rises behind the eastern mountains, after awakening to your original nature, it will rise in the west. Even though there is a difference between delusion and enlightenment, the original nature is fundamentally undifferentiated. Thus, the mind of all Buddhas is the mind of sentient beings, and the mind of sentient beings is the mind of all Buddhas. The mind is not two.

With a virtuous intention you have left your homes and come here. None of you came to the temple with an evil motivation. You all came here in order to awaken to the mind and transform your ordinary selves into Buddhas. So now, if you find that you are wasting your time—time as precious as gold—wouldn't this be very foolish? As the second hand of the clock moves, it always expounds the unsurpassable Dharma. Therefore, never think lightly of even a second or a minute. If you think, "Let's rest just for an hour or enjoy ourselves for thirty minutes," your practice will not improve. The ticking of the clock is showing you that you are always treading the path that leads to death. You do not know when your breath will cease. One hundred years of life is dependent upon a single breath that must renew itself every few seconds. When life might cease at any moment, can you afford to relax your minds by imagining that you will live for a very long time, and then spread yourselves out to sleep? If you act in such a way, liberation from birth and death will be very difficult indeed. Only when you have awakened can you sleep to your heart's content and enjoy yourselves as you wish. For then you will have transcended the limitations of time. Therefore, you must now practice truthfully and awaken truthfully. Someone who only meditates because others do so and then just wastes his time while sitting, is not really practicing.

Only after you have truthfully awakened can you fully appreciate the kindness of the Buddhas. For then you realize that all the Buddhas and patriarchs came to their awakening through enduring many hardships and by exerting tremendous efforts. The very appreciation of their kindness is the repayment of it. Thus, first of all, you will proceed to repay the kindness of the Buddhas.

Secondly, you will proceed to repay the debt to your almsgivers. For it is due to their kindness that you receive houses in which to live, food to eat, clothes to wear, and medicines for when you are ill. It is necessary that you repay the debts you have incurred in this way. Thirdly, you will proceed to benefit all sentient beings. Wouldn't it be joyful to do such things?

> All Buddhas teach the true Dharma of
>   non-doing.
> How marvelous it is when there is nothing
>   to gain and nothing to lose.
> Then, like a deaf man or a fool, one becomes
>   an unencumbered guest.
> Bright and clear, that which has no abode is
>   Vairocana Buddha.

When deluded people look inside themselves, they will find there are things to be cultivated and to be gained. Therefore, they make a great effort to practice. But as soon as they have completed what they set out to do, they realize that there was nothing really to have been done. Thus, the true Dharma involves non-doing. All things that are done will finally cease. Thus the Dharma of doing is the false Dharma. But everything that you do—which, in reality, is non-doing—constitutes eternal truth. Such actions will not cease even though you attempt to be finished with them. This is the truth of the unborn and undestroyed.

Therefore, all the Buddhas of the three times, all the patriarchs, the bodhisattvas, and the spiritual advisors of the present age have expounded and are expounding the Dharma that is no Dharma. If someone claims that something was said, this would be mistaken.

In this world all people look for the Dharma of doing, that is, for some thing. But the true Dharma is to look for the Dharma of non-doing. This is truly extraordinary.

Now two months of this winter retreat have passed and only one month remains. Therefore, I will introduce you to some words of advice of the ancient masters concerning "the careful examination of oneself during practice as a means to assist in one's awakening." Since you all claim to be practicing meditation, it is important to examine yourself in these ways while sitting.

1. *Are you aware of the heaviness of the four kinds of debt you are incurring?* These four great debts are (1) the money donated to build the temple, (2) the food donated to feed the monks, (3) the clothes made and given to the monks, and (4) the medicines prescribed at times of illness. Do you fully realize how deeply in debt you are? It has been said that each grain of rice offered out of sincere faith is as heavy as Mount Sumeru.

2. *Are you aware that with the passing of each thought this impure body composed of the four elements is decaying?* The body is composed of the four basic elements of earth, water, fire, and air. It is said to be impure because if you look inside it, you will find it to be composed of such things as urine, feces, blood, gastric juices, and bones. It is as though these things have been assembled together and put into a bag made out of skin. The breath then passes in and out of this bag. This is what we call a human body.

When such a body is healthy, you have the impression that you could live for a hundred or a thousand years. However, are you not aware that with the passing of each thought you are taking a step along the path that leads only to death? With every minute, every second, with each moment, time rushes on and propels you toward death.

3. *Do you realize that your life force depends upon each single breath?* No matter who you are, your life force is contained within each breath you take. A single inhalation and exhalation is equivalent to one hundred years. For if you exhale but are unable to inhale again, even a human life of one hundred years will come to an end.

4. *In this lifetime have you met the Buddhas and patriarchs?* Were you born at the time of the Buddha, then you could have met him. However, if in this lifetime you meet a spiritual advisor who practices meditation well, then this can be said to be equivalent to meeting one of the patriarchs. To encounter such beings is not the result of an insignificant karmic circumstance. On the contrary, it is due to karmic conditions that are only met with once every hundred million aeons.

5. *When you hear a discourse on the unsurpassable Dharma, do you appreciate how rare and precious this is?* In one of his previous lives the Buddha was born as a king. One day a *yaksa* (a cannibal spirit who lives on blood) appeared before him and said, "Since all conditioned things are impermanent, they are subject to production and destruction." Upon hearing these words of Dharma, the king was so delighted that he bowed down out of thanks to the *yaksa* and praised him for having expounded such a profound teaching. In response the *yaksa* said that there were other teachings that surpassed what he had already taught.

However, he was very hungry at the moment and would have to drink some warm blood before he could deliver them. The king immediately offered his own body for this purpose and the *yaksa* accepted it. However, since the king could only listen to the teaching while he was still alive, he suggested that he would climb to the top of a tall tree and, once the discourse was over, would leap down and thus make a sacrifice of his body. The *yaksa* agreed to this suggestion and the king then climbed to the top of a nearby tree.

The *yaksa* then said, "When production and destruction cease, Nirvana is happiness." When he heard these words the king was so delighted that he immediately jumped down from the tree soth at the *yaksa* could eat his body. But at this very moment, the *yaksa* was suddenly transformed into Indra, the king of the gods. He caught the king in his arms and praised him for disregarding his body for the sake of the Dharma.

Likewise, we too should have such a strong resolution when listening to the true Dharma. In this way we will proceed swiftly to the realization of Buddhahood.

6. *Do you stay within the monastery grounds and observe your moral precepts?* This question implies that you might transgress the precepts once outside the monastery. In general, it asks whether you are keeping your moral integrity. It has been said that "in the abode of the Buddhas, there are no enlightened beings who transgress their precepts, and behind the doors of Bodhidharma, there are no patriarchs who freely indulge in unwholesome deeds." To behave in an unwholesome manner is simply to behave like an ordinary sentient being. Thus, a person with such conduct would never win the respect of sentient beings. Even though he may have had a great enlightenment experience, without being respected he would be unable to be of any benefit to others. Therefore, it is important to keep your precepts pure

and understand how to maintain your moral integrity. Such a person is truly practicing meditation.

7. *Do you engage in unnecessary conversation with those who sit next to you?* The more you chatter, the more will delusive thoughts continue to arise unimpeded. Therefore, no progress will be made in your practice. Furthermore, you should not suggest to other meditators that they should go out and enjoy themselves, thus preventing them from meditating diligently.

8. *Do you incessantly create agitation by provoking arguments?* While practicing with a group of monks, are you in the habit of saying things to the others that give rise to arguments that even result in fights? If you inform someone of the bad things said about him by another, surely this would create the causes for quarrels and fighting. To agitate the minds of others with such behavior will only prevent them from practicing well.

9. *Is your* hwadu *bright, clear, and uninterrupted throughout the twenty-four hours of the day?* If your *hwadu* is really vivid and always present, then thoughts of going here and there and of enjoying yourself will have no opportunity to arise. It is because you do not hold the *hwadu* firmly that you always want to walk in the mountains and wander about aimlessly.

10. *Does your* hwadu *remain continuous and unbroken even during conversation?* When you are talking to someone and listening to what he has to say, your attention to the *hwadu* should never be interrupted. Even in the midst of such an exchange you should remain bright and vivid.

11. *In the face of adverse and favorable conditions, do your perceptions of seeing, hearing, feeling, etc., form a single mass?*

You should avoid falling prey to the lure of external circumstances. Instead try to keep your concentration of mind uniform and steady. All perceptions, whether of good or bad, of the universe or your own body, should maintain a uniform quality, thus uniting them in a single mass.

12. *When reflecting on yourself, are you confident that you will be able to surpass even the Buddhas and patriarchs?* When you reflect on how much progress you have made in your practice, do you think that your qualities will equal those of the Buddhas? In this way, you should ponder on how much your practice has advanced. Furthermore, do you consider that you can attain great enlightenment and thus become a respected and accomplished being?

13. *Are you confident that during this lifetime the wisdom of the Buddha will be definitely transmitted to you?* Do you think that you will be able to awaken or not? Do you intend to practice meditation until your wisdom becomes the same as that of the Buddhas?

14. *While your body is healthy and you are still able to go where you wish and sit in meditation, do you reflect on the sufferings of hell?* The sufferings of hell are not so very far away. Even while in good health, if you commit an unwholesome deed, the causes for the suffering of hell will be right there. But although you may be sick and bedridden, if you constantly and earnestly investigate the *hwadu* so that it remains unbroken, you will not go to hell. However, now that you are healthy, do you realize that if you commit an unwholesome deed, you will go to hell?

15. *With this body that is the fruition of past actions, will you be able to liberate yourself from endless transmigration within the cycle of birth and death?* Do you think that you will be able to attain liberation and thus free yourself from the sufferings

of birth and death? This body in its entirety is the result of actions that you have committed in the past. Moreover, the mind of each person is the Dharma body (*Dharmakaya*); the result of your past actions is the Fruition body (*Sambhoga-kaya*); and the performance of actions motivated by the mind is the Transformation body (*Nirmanakaya*). Each one of us is endowed in this way with the three bodies of the Buddha.

16. *Does your mind remain unmoved when subjected to the eight winds?* The eight winds are: gain, loss; fame, disrepute; praise, criticism; pleasure and displeasure. When you see pleasant or unpleasant things or when you are confronted by adverse or favorable conditions, do you always remain collected and undisturbed and keep your mind as steady as a mountain and as tranquil as the deep ocean?

These are sixteen methods of carefully examining oneself while practicing meditation. Furthermore, the ancients have said: "If you do not save yourself during this lifetime, in what other lifetime will you have the opportunity to do so?" If, after death, it were certain that you would be reborn with another human body, then there would be nothing wrong with just lying down and sleeping your time away during this life. However. it is not easy to find a human body. It is as difficult as for "a blind turtle to pass its head through a wooden yoke."

Imagine that there is a blind turtle living deep in the ocean. Every hundred years it comes to the surface in order to breathe. Occasionally, it accomplishes this by fortuitously passing its head through a wooden yoke floating on the surface and then resting it on the edge of the yoke. It would already be very difficult for a clear-sighted turtle to come up from so deep and pass its head through the yoke floating in the middle of the ocean. How much more difficult would it be for a blind turtle. It is just as difficult to find a human body. Thus, if someone obtains such a precious human body but only lives idly and dies without having achieved anything, then he will have squandered his life. There could be no greater waste than that.

Now only one month remains until the end of this retreat. Soon it will be the lunar New Year. At this time you may want to just idly enjoy yourselves and thus waste your time. However, if you behave like this, your life will be of no purpose and you will die in vain. Therefore, during this last month, you must practice diligently and exert much effort. Within this time, you must resolve the great matter of birth and death

SIXTH LECTURE (Given in Conjunction with a Memorial Ceremony)

(*After ascending the Dharma seat the master calls the name of the deceased and strikes his staff on the base of his seat.*)

With this I strike and destroy the innumerable karmic hindrances of all sentient beings.
(*He strikes his staff a second time.*)

With this I destroy any fixed opinions of enlightened beings concerning their attainments.
(*He strikes his staff a third time.*)

With this I expose the original face of the deceased. Do you all understand this principle or not?

Hak!

Through melting gold a bowl can be made of which the shape can differ in a thousand ways. However, the nature of gold never changes.

Today's lecture is that of the last day of the twelfth month of the lunar year. At the same time, it is for the benefit of a deceased person. Thus I venture to ask this assembly: Where is the way to Nirvana for this deceased man? The light of the jewel moon of the Dharma ocean pervades the entire universe. Do you understand this principle or not?

> To dismiss the old year and welcome in
>   the new is to pass the year of the donkey.
> Even though there is no increase or decrease,
>   the four seasons return.
> Three countless aeons pass by at the very
>   moment when delusion in the mind
>   is brought to an end.
> Thus, quiescent and tranquil, without doing
>   anything, one attains Nirvana.

Today is the last day of the last month for all of you gathered here as well as for the deceased. What does this last day of the year represent? It stands for the moment when the light of the eyes falls to the ground [when one dies]. For all of you, the time will come when the light of your eyes will fall to the ground. It has already happened to the deceased. In reality, there is no such thing as the year of the donkey within the twelve-year calendric cycle. Likewise, you dismiss the old year and welcome in the new one, thus giving the impression that something has happened. In reality, nothing has happened. For all of you as well as for the deceased, there is fundamentally no birth and death. Thus, there is no increase nor decrease. Nothing is born, nothing passes away. However, the four seasons always return. Furthermore, it is said that a Buddha realizes Buddhahood after practicing for three countless aeons. However, the three countless aeons will pass by at the very moment when all of you here or the deceased cut through the delusions of the mind. At that time, being tranquil and inactive, being unconcerned with either birth and death, or coming and going, or past and present, or dismissing the old year and welcoming in the new, you attain Nirvana.

O departed one! If you say that you have been born, it

would be like talking of bubbles floating on the surface of water. If you say that you have passed away, it would be like saying that smoke is drifting over the mountains. Therefore, all of you monks gathered here, say something for the benefit of the deceased! What is the principle beyond birth and death? What happens when the bubbles disappear and the smoke has vanished? That is to say, when this body has not been born and has not yet died, where does the mind abide?

(*The assembly remains silent.*)

Since you do not say anything, then I will do so instead. One fine ray of light from the curl of hair between the Buddha's eyes transcends past, present, and future. In addition, it pervades the ten directions throughout the universe. Although the lotus emerges out of mud, it is not sullied by dirt.

O departed one! Since it is said that you have left this world, today a one-hundredth-day ceremony is indeed being performed for you. However, is there really any birth and death or not? The body is illusory, it is like a dream. All of us must wake up from this dream. Someone who has not been able to awaken to the mind, whether he sleeps or is awake, is still dreaming. Although the body is not real, we are under the illusion that it is. Therefore, we are said to be dreaming. Why do we dream in this way? This is because of our being conditioned by habitual tendencies. Thereby we succumb to this illusion and have to endure endless suffering. Thus we seem to undergo birth and death. However, this is just like an image appearing in a mirror, which, in a similar way, seems to exist when in fact it does not. Likewise, we succumb to the illusion that we are seeing something that in fact is not there. However, the subtle substance of the true nature is intrinsically pure in itself. It does not follow this body into birth, nor does it cease upon its death. All actions arise due to previous conditions just like flames spring forth from snow and ice.

Throughout beginningless aeons, since even before the creation of the Earth, the original nature is bright and clear. So when can there be birth and death? In reality, there has been no death for the deceased. So even if some claim that he has died, what real need is there to offer him guidance today? Because in the case where the illusion remains that he has died, the principle of the undying is thereby shown. But truly, when could you die? When could you be born?

When coming, there is no place from which to come. When going, although it may seem that you are going somewhere, there is really no place to which to go. Originally, you have never come from anywhere. Therefore, there can be no place to which you can go. Hence, in itself, the true nature is always thus. And this is the path to the Nirvana of the Buddhas. This is the original face of the deceased. This is the place where the bodies and the minds of all of you gathered here are at peace. Thus you can go as you wish to the celestial realms or to the Buddha worlds. You can freely wander everywhere. How joyful! Indeed how joyful!

SEVENTH LECTURE

Today is the beginning of the free season. Free season (Korean: *Haejae*, lit., "release from restriction") actually implies the realization of your own true nature and the continuation of the wisdom of the Buddhas and the patriarchs. Furthermore, it only becomes a genuine release from restriction when you are able to compassionately guide and help other beings. If there is anyone here who has reached such a state, then say something!

(*The assembly remains silent.*)

Since no one says anything, now it cannot really be the free season. So what excuse do you have for idly enjoying yourselves, relaxing and thus wasting your time?

Having been unable to enter the mysterious
     gateway of the patriarchs but nevertheless
     being proud
Is like trying to cross the ocean on the back
     of a mosquito. Surely this would be
     self-deception.
To presumptuously claim to have seen
     one's true nature
Would be like saying that one has bound
     Mount Chogye with spider webs.

Those who noisily proclaim to be awakened only succeed
in deceiving themselves and cheating the sages. Such lies
are as futile as trying to bind Mount Chogye with spider
webs. And those who, without having been able to awaken,
just enjoy themselves and wander here and there are like
people trying to cross the ocean by riding mosquitoes. Do
you think that anyone could ever succeed in either binding
Mount Chogye with spider webs or crossing the ocean on
a mosquito? By deceiving yourself in such a way, how
could your life not be in vain and your death full of distress? Therefore, you should never pretend to have awakened when in fact you have not.

Your sole task is to search for the subtle Nirvanic mind
of all Buddhas in the midst of the mind of yourself, a sentient being. This means that by cultivating the mind you
have as a sentient being, you will finally discover the subtle
Nirvanic mind of all Buddhas. You should not search for
it elsewhere.

Birth and death are indeed a great matter. But life is
highly unstable and transient. For being unable to inhale
one simple breath will mark the end of a human life that
may have endured for a hundred years. Since the continuity of life depends upon each single breath, how can
you ever know when you will die? If death only afflicted
the old and not the young, then, being assured of many

years ahead, you could with justification lie down and just sleep comfortably. But this is not the case. Birth and death are a great matter.

Life passes swiftly by. So how can you permit yourself to behave in a wild, uncontrolled manner? When the light of your eyes falls to the ground at death, regrets will be completely in vain. At that time, conscious at last that you will soon die, you may start worrying about what to do. But then whatever you may try and do will be of no use.

Throughout beginningless aeons the Way has been obscured by the great weight and depth of defilements. Exactly how heavy and deep are these defilements? They are as heavy as the earth and as deep as the ocean. Defilements are actually the habitual tendencies you have acquired since beginningless time. Since they are so deeply ingrained within you and weigh you down so greatly, how can you not see the need to practice with the utmost diligence? The defilements are like clouds covering the sun. Although the sun shines brightly behind the clouds, its brightness cannot be seen. Only when the clouds disperse will its brilliance be clearly apparent.

Now if you really want to unearth a precious gem from the mud and stones of defilements, you should think of how snow and ice harden and melt. Recently there has been much snow here. Now it has packed and hardened on the ground and will not melt very quickly. Just look! The snow is delivering an unsurpassable discourse on Dharma. For to dissolve the defilements and discover your true nature is similar to the melting of this snow. In order for it to melt it must be exposed to the sun. Thereupon it turns into water, which you can then use for drinking, washing, and so forth. Imagine how long it would take to melt if it were only exposed to the sun for one day and then allowed to harden again over the following ten cold days. It is similar when you try to practice meditation. If you practice hard for one day but then relax and enjoy yourselves during the next ten days, how will the hardened crust of the defilements ever melt?

Even in the midst of the utmost quiescence, you should never let the *hwadu* fade. For if at such times it remains bright and vivid, then great awakening will draw nearer. Furthermore, the meditator should now consider the *hwadu* as his very life. When coming, the *hwadu* should be coming. When going, the *hwadu* should be going. While eating, the *hwadu* should be eating. And even while defecating, it should be the *hwadu* that defecates. If you practice in such a way, then great awakening will certainly be closer. Therefore, do not just idly enjoy yourselves to no purpose! Carefully and earnestly investigate the living word [the *hwadu*].

In conclusion I would like to comment upon this well-known proverb.

> In the utmost softness lies the greatest strength;
> In the utmost harmony, the sublimest joy;
> In the utmost gentleness, the noblest virtue;
> And in the utmost meekness, the highest
>   felicity.
> Only with the utmost patience does one
>   become a sage.

It is possible that someone might appear on the outside to be rather simple and even foolish. He may seem to have no courage, to be overly compliant and slow witted. However, inside he may be yielding a mighty sword. Similarly, when confronting circumstances, on the outside you should appear to deal with them softly and compliantly, yet inside your mind should be as sharp as a mighty sword. A person who can act in such a way has truly built up a sound practice.

Likewise, you should try to be harmonious. You should

learn to like and get on well with one another, and to do things for other people instead of yourself. But if you behave in a way that is contrary to the well-being and interests of others, then you will only create conflict.

It is important to be gentle and not to go against the wishes of others. Even go out of your way to be helpful to other people. In this way you will amass the noblest of virtues.

Meekness is another quality that should be cultivated. Instead of forcing yourselves on others you should learn to flexibly adapt yourselves to their needs. You should listen well to what they say and offer to help them in whatever work they are doing. In this way you will find contentment and happiness.

Finally, you must learn to be patient. You need to be able to forbear hardships, endure difficulties and undertake what is arduous. While practicing, you are liable to encounter difficult periods. It is important not to give up at such times but to bear through them diligently. In this way the strength of forbearance will grow within you and in the end you will become accomplished sages. Such people are able to sit on the lion throne and utter a lion's roar for the welfare of all beings.

INFORMAL LECTURE I

I would like to recount to you an incident that occured to me in the year in which I became a monk [1938]. I had just spent the summer meditation season in Samil Am meditation hall at Songgwang Sa with twenty-two other monks. It had been a fruitful season, since I had put a great deal of effort into my practice to the point where I no longer cared whether I lived or died. During this time I had become a friend in the Way with a monk called Paeksan Sunim. He was a very serious meditator. Even while walking he would keep his eyes half-closed and never look around him.

When the free season arrived, Paeksan Sunim and myself decided to leave Songgwang Sa and go elsewhere to continue our practice. However, Soktu Sunim, the teacher of my own teacher, had recently asked me to stay and be his attendant. Thus I was of two minds as to what I should do. One morning, immediately after breakfast, Paeksan Sunim decided to leave. Although I wanted to go with him, I felt that I should heed the request of Soktu Sunim. So he left alone. The morning passed and, having given much thought to my predicament, by lunch time I decided that it would have been better after all if I had left. So, shortly after lunch, I put my knapsack on my back and left to follow Paeksan Sunim.

To catch up with my friend I had to reach Taean Sa temple near the town of Koksong, which was about seventy *li* (30 km) away. I walked steadily during the afternoon but as night fell there were still ten *li* to go. Not knowing the way, I decided to spend the night in a nearby village. During the night I began to feel very ill. This sudden sickness may have been due to the fact that I had simply over-exerted myself. Throughout the summer I had strenuously pursued my practice and, with hardly a break, had just walked sixty *li* in one afternoon carrying a heavy knapsack. The next morning, after the villagers had given me something to eat, I nevertheless continued on my way in spite of the illness. However, my body was racked with pain and, with much difficulty, it took me the entire morning to cover the remaining ten *li*. I finally reached Taean Sa at midday.

I met Paeksan Sunim at the gate of the temple. He had eaten lunch and was just about to leave for a short walk. Instead he welcomed me inside. Then, after eating lunch, I had to lie down because of the pain my body was still causing me. For the rest of the afternoon I was able to rest.

By then it had started raining and we were unable to go out anyway. However, my illness persisted through the night and into the following morning.

By early morning the rain finally cleared up. But I still felt too sick to continue traveling that day and thought it better to stay in the temple to rest. Shortly, a note came to us from the temple administration announcing that the rain had stopped. This obviously meant that the monks in the temple thought it was time for us to leave. After discussing this matter with Paeksan Sunim we realized that we had no choice but to go. Because I felt so weak and ill, I was at first rather reluctant to set out upon the road. But my friend explained that it would be most troublesome for us to stay any longer.

You have to remember that the situation in the temples was quite different in those days from what it is now. This was the time when married priests were in charge of most of the temples. Nowadays if a meditating monk wished to stay on an extra day because he was too sick to travel, the temple administration could never object. But then it was not possible for us meditators to challenge anything that the married priests said.

So now I started to reflect upon my situation. For more than a day I had been literally moaning in illness. My whole body, from the top of my head to the soles of my feet, was in pain. However, I thought, a monk practices in order to attain liberation from birth and death and should not be upset by physical pain. And, in reality, where was this pain that had been causing me such suffering? Where was it located? In this way I carefully searched throughout my body for the place of illness. While pursuing this inner search for the pain, I suddenly realized that there was no single place where any pain was located. Although I had scrutinized my entire body from head to toe, I could find no particular pain anywhere. Thereupon I was immediately cured.

Straightaway I sprang to my feet and told Paeksan Sunim that I was now completely cured and we could continue on our way. However, at that moment the bell was rung for lunch. So we stayed to eat and left shortly after the meal. That afternoon we walked without difficulty to the town of Koksong and spent the night at a temple in the town. The next day too we continued on our journey.

This account illustrates how important it is for a meditator to maintain a firm hold on his mind. This is the duty of every cultivator of the Way. The mind is as wily as a fox and as mischievous as a goblin. If we just let it be, it will give rise to all kinds of different thoughts. One should not allow this to happen. Instead, if we make a firm decision in our minds, all delusive thoughts can be washed away. In this way, those of us who claim to practice meditation should keenly poise our minds like a very sharp dagger. Thus should we bear ourselves with wisdom.

To succeed in the practice of meditation, you must raise the final resolve. So what is this final resolve? It is true that all of you here have left your families with the resolve to cultivate your minds. So now you carry the knapsack of a monk and spend your lives in the meditation hall. But this is just an ordinary resolve. It is not what is meant by the final resolve.

The final resolve is to completely sever all concerns about life and death so that you no longer care whether you live or die. With such a resolve, a meditator just sticks the two words life and death to his forehead and, grinding his teeth, perseveres with his practice. When so determined, he casts aside the body just as he would throw a stone into the gutter.

Why is it necessary to exert such effort? Because the Buddhas and patriarchs of the past as well as the wise teachers of today have all said the same thing, namely: "Every sentient being is intrinsically a Buddha." But, reflecting on yourselves now, do you have the confidence to truly say that you are a noble and enlightened Buddha? Is there anyone here who would claim to be a Buddha?

If you feel that you are not yet a Buddha, this means that the downfall of the six thieves is still to take place. All things in the external world that pass through the six sense doors are like thieves who are intent on cheating you. They continuously deceive you and drag you here and there. And as soon as you are deceived in even the slightest way by one of these thieves, it is equivalent to being killed by them. For at that moment they take control of your mind. Because of them, intrinsic Buddhas are made to act like ordinary sentient beings.

In the face of these six thieves, you need the courage of a soldier on the front line fighting the enemy. When suddenly faced with an enemy in the midst of a battle, a soldier does not have the time to ponder whether his adversary can shoot well or not, or whether such a shot would be fatal. In order not to risk being killed by the enemy's fire, he is simply forced to shoot immediately. Similarly, as soon as the slightest thought appears in the doorway of one of the six senses, you should be as alarmed as though a thief were trying to break into your house. The moment one of the six thieves shows itself in the doorway of the senses, the *hwadu* investigation of the essential will have deserted you. Otherwise, how could one of the thieves have appeared in the first place? For as long as the *hwadu* is held firmly in mind, the six sense doors will be kept tightly closed and there will be no gap through which a thief could enter. Therefore, while the *hwadu* remains vivid, you remain alive. But as soon as one of the six thieves manages to enter the door of the senses, you are already dead.

In order to cause the downfall of the six thieves you must cast aside all concern for the body. You should discard it as you would a useless stone that serves no purpose. Habitually you blindly follow your uncontrolled attachment to the body and thus spend your entire lives trying to feed it and clothe it well, thereby making sure that it is comfortable. Throughout beginningless aeons you have been the servant of the body and have thus played the role of an ordinary sentient being. But from now on you should learn to make it serve you. Likewise, instead of being captivated by the six senses, you should also make them obey you. Henceforth it is you who must have the final word. In this way your practice will be able to progress well.

It is a great mistake to think that after having practiced hard for a few days you are then entitled to lie back and enjoy yourself for a while. It is easy to find any number of pretexts for behaving in this manner. But to do so will cause you to be killed by the six thieves. Thus you will be reduced to playing the role of a corpse.

Therefore, when practicing meditation, it is most important to raise the final resolve. Otherwise, it will not be possible to pierce through the barrier of the patriarchs. Through your practice you are not searching for anything far away from yourself. On the contrary, you are seeking nothing but your own original nature. Thus, this is a task that each of you must accomplish on your own. But if you lack the final resolve, it will take immeasurable aeons to make any progress.

There are many people who, after persevering in their practice for a while, do not feel that they are progressing. They then give up in despair and start to think about practicing something else. In this way they succumb to delusive thinking and laziness. However, such an attitude is self-destructive. For if you were sure of being reborn as a human being, then it would not matter so much if you wasted this one life in idly enjoying yourselves. But actually there is no certainty as to what sort of rebirth is awaiting you.

Some people believe that death is final and there is no further life after it. Such persons are regarded as having fallen into the extreme view of nihilism. Then there are others who are unconcerned about the nature of their subsequent rebirths. They think that now one should just enjoy this life and if one is then reborn in hell or as an animal, what does it really matter? They believe that since the mind is eternal one will continue to receive numerous bodies, what reason is there to be concerned about any particular rebirth? People who think in this way fall into the extreme view of eternalism. It is important to free yourselves from these two extremes of nihilism and eternalism.

After practicing meditation for some time you will experience entering the door of emptiness. Subsequently you have to take one further step off the hundred-foot pole. Only then will you be able to pierce through the barrier of the patriarchs. Now what does it really mean, to "pierce through" this barrier? It means to transcend the two extremes of nihilism and eternalism. This is achieved because at such a time when one thought arises, all the ten thousand forms of the universe come into being; and when one thought ceases, they all return to quiescent emptiness, and the joy of Nirvana is experienced.

It is still possible that even after repeated hard practice it may seem that no progress is being made. At such times the thought may occur that you are simply not suited for such an arduous and difficult task. Such a practice of meditation may be suitable for those who have already had a great deal of experience in the past, but not for a beginner like oneself. But to entertain such thoughts is to crush the seed of Buddhahood. It is like digging a hell for yourself. To reject this task simply because it seems difficult will only cause you to undergo further suffering wherever you are. To give up in this way will leave you far removed from awakening. The path ahead of you will grow dim and you will be destined to endless days of darkness. In such a state, how will you ever be able to free yourself from birth and death?

No matter how difficult it may seem at times, if you continue uninterruptedly to exert yourselves, your meditation will eventually mature. The defilements you have accumulated will gradually disappear and your wandering thoughts will lessen. In this way, progress will become visible. As long as you maintain a sustained effort, why should you not finally awaken?

The Buddhas and the patriarchs of the past were ordinary human beings like yourselves. It was only through their strong determination that they were able to endure beyond strength what was hard to endure and thus succeeded in accomplishing the difficult task of awakening. The method of practice has not changed. It is the same now as it was then.

However, it is common nowadays for people to say that their practice does not progress well because it is now the Dharma-ending age, a time when the teachings of Buddhism are declining. Such talk is foolish. Whether at the time of the Buddha or nowadays, as soon as the thought has arisen to realize Buddhahood through searching for the mind, one enters the supreme vehicle. Even if someone should have thought at the time of the Buddha that this task was too difficult for an ordinary sentient being, then he too would have made no progress. For such a person, the Dharma-ending age would have been upon him.

Nowadays, civilization in the East and the West is said to be at a turning point. Every moment is a time of great uncertainty. If a third world war were to start, for example, no one could predict the outcome for the future of mankind. When such turmoil is present in human society, there is always the possibility that a change in direction can take place. Not only can individual nations undergo such changes, but even the ideologies of man as a whole can change. Such a time presents an especially good opportunity for your practice of meditation to progress. The world situation being so precarious, we feel impelled to practice out of the awareness that we can never tell at what moment we may die. In general, every time of great change and upheaval, such as the founding or the collapse of a nation, is very suitable for the successful practice of meditation.

It is important that you cultivate a strong desire to be of benefit to mankind. Such aspiration arises out of compassion. To be motivated by compassion for others produces a much stronger determination to practice than the simple wish to obtain your own liberation from birth and death. In this way you should earnestly devote yourselves to meditation even at the peril of your own life.

Furthermore, in order to be able to actually help others, you should seek to emulate the spirit of a great hero. This is necessary because only one who is the greatest hero among heroes is able to accomplish this difficult task. You need supreme courage in order to bring this practice to its completion. To transform this world into a Pure Land and to change ordinary sentient beings into accomplished sages is no easy matter. It is truly the work of a great hero.

INFORMAL LECTURE II

There are three essential elements of *hwadu* meditation: great faith, great courage, and great questioning. First, there is faith. This is not the faith of believing in the Buddha, but the faith you have in yourself. You must believe in yourself because all the Buddhas of the three times, all the patriarchs, the bodhisattvas, and the spiritual advisors of this generation have stated that each sentient being is originally a Buddha. Since the Buddha's words are not lies, it is certain that each person is fundamentally a Buddha.

Reflect on this: have you become a Buddha or not?

All the Buddhas made great efforts while practicing in order to attain Buddhahood. It was not achieved easily. When other people have become enlightened, think of yourself and of the fact that you have not yet been able to realize Buddhahood. Other people have become Buddhas but you have not. You just continue creating karma within the turning wheel of birth and death. From such thoughts, an attitude of self-reproach can be produced: "Why have I been unable to become a Buddha?"

Throughout beginningless aeons you have lived believing the body to be the self. You have just spent your time trying to feed, take care of, and protect it alone. A human being is composed of both a body and a mind. But you have completely disregarded the mind and only know the body, which is just a potential corpse. For thousands of years, you have only been thinking of protecting this thing that will eventually die. In this process attachment has been produced. You continually cling to good things and reject bad things. This is deluded thinking. As you continue in this manner, deluded thinking becomes stronger and stronger and appears to be your primary nature. You confuse deluded thinking for the mind. These days people say: "That which feels, isn't that the mind?" But to see and to feel is just the mind reacting according to circumstances. This is just deluded thinking. I will explain further. Taking the example of water: when it is still, the shining moon reflects in it. But if the water encounters certain conditions, such as the wind blowing, waves will arise. Then the moon cannot be clearly seen in it. Its reflection is broken up by the waves. Could you consider this to be an analogy for the mind? No, this would just be a "water-ripple" mind.

Confucian scholars speak about being good or bad by nature, meaning that a person's fundamental nature can be either good or bad. They think that these are the words of a great doctrine. But they are not. Why? Because, according to circumstances, if good conditions prevail, a good-natured mind arises; if bad conditions prevail, an ill-natured mind arises. A good-natured or an ill-natured mind originally has no fixed rules. The minds which arise according to circumstances are all forms of deluded thinking. Both a good mind and a bad mind are equally deluded thinking. Before a good or a bad mind arises, what is the mind like?

While in the United States at the Claremont School of Theology, a professor asked me, "What is it that knows how to see and hear? Isn't that the mind?" I answered, "You can call it the mind, but it is just a form of deluded thinking. What is the mind before you see or hear?" He said, "Surely, there is just nothing at all." I replied, "If you were sitting without thinking, would you be dead?" "No, I wouldn't," he answered. In conclusion I said, "If you wouldn't be a dead person, then there must be mind. What is the mind itself? You should look for it and awaken to it." In response he said that he would try and meditate on it.

As practitioners of meditation you know how to raise your fist or blink your eyes, how to eat rice or drink water. Isn't that thing it? So, before raising your fist or blinking your eyes, what is that thing? Without fail you must try and say something before a single thought arises. You must be clear about that thing. If you just wonder whether or not it is that which knows how to feel, then you don't really know what it is. Such an approach is called intellectual Zen.

To accomplish this task it is also necessary to produce an attitude of great courage. All people try to take good care of the body. Even though it is just a potential corpse they feed it well, clothe it well, and make it comfortable. During immeasurable aeons they have obeyed it and protected it. But by so doing they have only created much karma within the turning wheel of birth and death. Now it is important to make the body obey us. Once you have produced an attitude of great courage, you no longer know even how to sleep or eat. You completely forget everything and just practice meditation.

Moreover, you must cultivate great questioning. Whether you are contemplating "What is this?" or "No!" or "the cypress in the courtyard," if you just sit motionless, maintaining the *hwadu* without questioning and continuity, it will be just like "watching the tree, waiting for the rabbit." There was once a man who was walking through the woods. A rabbit scurried by, ran head first into a tree and thereby killed itself. The man then took it home and ate it. He then thought that the tree must be a special rabbit-catching tree. So he started to come back to see if there were any more dead rabbits. But no matter how long he waited, what probability would there be of another rabbit dying there? Similarly, if you just sit, keeping the *hwadu* with neither continuity nor inquiry, no progress will be made in meditation.

The Buddha held up a lotus flower. What did he mean by this? Zhaozhou said, "No!" For what reason? "The cypress in the courtyard." What is the meaning of such words? You fail to understand these things. Thus, you start questioning because you don't understand. If you understood, there would be no need for any questioning. In this practice, a meditator's greatest disease is to lack such questioning.

Some time ago I had the following experience. There was a monk by the name of Popch'un Sunim who was very diligent in his practice of meditation. Being companions in the Way, we were once traveling and practicing together. One time we went to stay in Sudo Am hermitage for a while. There was another monk staying there by the name of Chongdam Sunim, who was always very helpful to other people. As a means of developing compassion, he took the job of cleaning the toilet every day. However, one day he came down with dysentery, seemingly as a result of working in the toilet. He became so ill that he appeared to be close to death. As the hermitage was very remote and isolated, no medicine was available. He decided that if he were to die, he would die; and if he were to live, he would live. However, he learned of a raw food diet and after trying it for a few days, he was cured of his dysentery.

Later, the three of us left together in order to attend to some business. We reached the city of Sangju in the morning and ate lunch there. After lunch, Popch'un Sunim had great pains in his stomach. He couldn't even sit and was pacing back and forth. We went all over the city in search of different kinds of Oriental and Western medicine. We bought some but they did not help. Finally, Popch'un Sunim's stomach ruptured. In the city of Sangju, there were no hospital facilities where he could have undergone an operation. We took him to a doctor who told us to go to Taegu, but it was Sunday and too late in the evening to leave. We decided to go the following morning. Overnight I took him to the house of a friend of mine. We had him lie down to rest on the warm floor. He was sighing in distress, "I am going to die." Then he turned to me and said, "However, please practice well and ferry me across to the other shore of enlightenment." I replied, "It is the nature of our way of life as monks to be aware of the impermanence of existence. Therefore, we must be prepared for our departure at any moment. Besides this, there is nothing more I can really say. But as far as the relationship between friends on the path is concerned, we should try to assist one another from one life to the next. If I realize enlightenment first, I shall help to ferry you across and vice versa. In that case, you would not have to worry. Now, let's wait for the night to pass."

As usual we got up in the early morning around three o'clock. Chongdam Sunim came into the room and noticed how dark Popch'un Sunim's face had become. Popch'un Sunim asked why the room was so dark. In fact, it was his sight that was failing. His stomach was so painful that one couldn't even put one's hand on it. Around six o'clock, he passed away. Nothing could have been done. We had tried to get various medicines. A specialist had come to examine him. He had said that as the stomach had ruptured, the next morning between six and nine o'clock would be the most critical time. As it turned out, the doctor clearly had known what he was talking about.

Shortly afterwards we performed all the funeral rites and the cremation. This kind of work has to be done by ourselves and not by others. In fact, cultivators of the Way must know how to do all kinds of work. While living in Songgwang Sa, I myself perform the funeral rites if a monk happens to die. Since I have been here, it has happened about eight times.

In reality, we do not know at what moment we will die. When we are healthy, we believe that we will be able to live for a hundred years. To believe this is to deceive ourselves.

After the cremation, Chongdam Sunim and I disposed of Popch'un Sunim's remains. I had suggested to Chongdam Sunim that he come back with me to practice in Sudo Am. However, he had decided to go to Paekch'on Am hermitage. So I went back alone to Sudo Am with the firm resolution to practice diligently until the forty-ninth-day memorial ceremony. Within that time I hoped to awaken in order to be able to ferry Popch'un Sunim across. We were three companions in the Way, traveling together; one left this world, one went to a different temple. How did I feel then? At such times one's heart deeply experiences impermanence. To say that this body lives means very little. Do you realize that it depends upon each moment? In one minute we breathe in and out seventeen or eighteen times. The time of one breath is around three and a half seconds. Three and a half, three and a half, three and a half. . . . In one hour we breathe in and out one thousand and twenty times. Thus we can say that in one hour the life of a person begins and ends one thousand and twenty times. It is like the flame of an oil lamp in the wind or like the morning dew on the grass. We bear this precarious life within us but do not know at what moment we will die. In such a situation can we feel at ease? Therefore, you must awaken before you die.

At that time in Sudo Am, I was in charge of the kitchen. It was my responsibility to supply the provisions to be used by the community of monks. Even though I had decided to practice diligently, I still had to spend much time taking care of the kitchen supplies. When I had finally finished this work, only eight days remained before the forty-ninth-day ceremony. So I told the monks to take care of things as they saw best, since I really had to go and meditate.

I went to stay in a small cabin behind the hermitage. A young monk brought me my morning and noon meals, since I intended to practice without going down to the main hermitage. However, since I had been so busy, much of the concentration I had developed through my previous hard practice had dissipated. When I sat, I often dozed, and the practice did not go well. This went on for two days, leaving me with only six days within which to awaken in order to ferry Popch'un Sunim across by the ceremony day. With so little time left, I could not continue with such poor practice. I decided to do "standing on the toes" meditation. So, with the palms of my hands together, I meditated standing on my toes. By meditating in this way, drowsiness could not interrupt me as it had before. For days and nights I stood like this. I would only sit to eat my meals when they were brought. Then, once again, with my palms together, I would resume the meditation standing on my toes. In such standing meditation the hardest part is to get over the first two hours. After this, the main difficulties are overcome. Whether sitting, lying, or standing, one's meditation continues unaffected as soon as the mind is settled in concentration. Consequently, I felt neither tiredness nor pain in my legs as I was pursuing this practice.

On the day of the memorial ceremony, around three o'clock in the afternoon, Popch'un Sunim appeared to me. He was wearing a traditional hat, holding a wooden staff and carrying a monk's knapsack on his back. He said, "I came to visit you as it is the forty-ninth day." I just continued practicing. Even though it was the forty-ninth day, I did not go down for the ceremony. As I had not been able to awaken, what would have been the use of going? The monks there performed the ceremony, but I just continued meditating.

On the seventh day of this standing meditation, as it was approaching nine o'clock, the clock made a loud click before striking the hour. Upon hearing that click "one thought turned back." On that occasion I chanted the following stanza:

> One single sound: the three thousand worlds are
> swallowed up.
> This fellow appears alone and shouts "Ha"
> nine times.
> The ticking of the clock is but the all-embracing
> exposition of the teaching.
> Piece by piece the metal and the wood are but
> the pure Dharma body.

This was one time when I put effort into my practice in order to ferry a friend across.

Such intense standing practice served to remove the obstructions caused by torpor and restlessness. The effect was like the experience of a clear sky completely free of clouds. It instantaneously allowed me to enter and abide at the original place. Thus I was enabled to pass over a very difficult step. You can only do such continuous standing meditation with the thought, "It doesn't matter if I die."

It takes much more than just a feeble effort to endure such practice for seven days. But if you try with a sense of great urgency, then awakening comes about quickly. There are no fixed rules saying that you must spend many decades before awakening. If you raise a strong resolve and persevere with great effort, the practice will rapidly progress. If you put little effort into the practice without any sense of urgency, awakening will take immeasurable aeons.

CHAPTER SEVEN

Advice and Encouragement

> *Beneath blue clouds*
> *A white crane is perched*
> *On the branch of an aging pine.*
> *Do you enjoy*
> *The embroidery of rivers and mountains*
> *Shining with autumn colour?*
> *Let's bask together*
> *In the subtle fragrance*
> *Of the wild chrysanthemum.*

As the basis for giving, it is important to cultivate an attitude of all-pervading loving kindness. This should not be directed solely to humans but to all the various sentient beings. With such an attitude we should try to freely give what we have without any feelings of regret.[14]

There are three kinds of giving. The first is to give by means of your understanding of Dharma. This means to devote yourself to the service of others by realizing, for their sake, the emptiness of your own self and your desires. The second is to give away your material possessions without any reluctance. To give with attachment produces merit that is stained by defilement. Only when giving is free from attachment is the resultant merit undefiled. We should learn to give readily and without hesitation with the same ease as when giving away cold water or a dirty mop.

The third kind of giving is to give without apprehension. If, due to your merit and wisdom, you are able to give your body and mind without apprehension, then this will produce great loving kindness and compassion in which yourself and others are seen without any differentiation.

There is a well-known story of the Buddha in which, during one of his previous lives as a bodhisattva, he sacrificed his own body to feed a starving tigress and her cubs. Now, if we regret having to give away even a couple of dollars when asked, how would we feel if it came to giving away even our own body? However, we should recall that, according to the law of karma, the offering of this present body that we hold so dear to us will result in our receiving a far superior one in the future. Moreover, if we can give it away without any attachment to form, we will ultimately be able to receive the greatest reward—the fruit of Buddhahood. The Buddha was able to reach such a level of accomplishment because, while accumulating merit, he could give away not only material possessions, but even his mind and body without any regret or apprehension.

It has been said that "the vessel of morality must be pure in order for the water of concentration to be so clear that the moon of wisdom can be reflected brightly within it." Similarly your body can be compared with a vessel that is to be filled with Dharma.

To keep the body pure means to observe the moral precepts. To imagine that you can succeed in the practice of meditation while disregarding your precepts is like thinking you can fill a steamer with water. Because a steamer has many holes at the bottom, any water you pour in will just run out again. Likewise, someone who tries to meditate without observing the precepts causes his vessel of Dharma to break. Therefore, only by keeping the precepts will your Dharma vessel remain intact.

When Bodhidharma came to China, people at that time thought that the practice of Buddhism merely entailed the observance of morality and the study of sutras. For this reason Bodhidharma said, "To only practice morality is to be bewitched by heavenly beings. To spend one's time reading sutras is outside of the true Way. To just recite the Buddha's name is to fall under the influence of Mara." Although the simple observance of morality and the recitation of Amitabha's name may cause you to be reborn in a heavenly realm, they are not practices that are able to liberate you from birth and death. And although the study of sutras is a Buddhist practice, it is only a secondary vehicle and not the principal one. The principal vehicle is to search for the mind and awaken to it. For this reason, Bodhidharma disregarded the mere observance of precepts and the study of words and letters and emphasized the practice of meditation. His teaching is one of "pointing directly to the mind of man, seeing one's own original nature and becoming a Buddha."

Nevertheless, one consequence of practicing meditation well is that you will naturally come to observe the precepts of moral discipline. Why is this? Let us recall the first five basic precepts: to refrain from killing, stealing, sexual misconduct, lying, and drinking intoxicants. How could your practice possibly progress well if you were engaged in any of these five actions? Therefore, when trying to cultivate your mind, you will quite naturally come to observe the precepts.

Therefore, not only does the observance of the moral precepts provide a sound basis for meditation, but meditation, in turn, strengthens your practice of morality. The two—moral discipline and meditation—should be developed together so that they may mutually assist one another. They are like the two wings of a bird. If either one is lacking, the bird will be unable to fly.

At the outset of your practice, it is essential to observe the precepts while endeavoring to cultivate concentration and wisdom. Only when the practice has been brought to completion do such states as "non-cultivation" and "non-realization" occur. At these stages, the entire universe is seen to be the pure body of Vairocana Buddha. At such a time, because birth and death have come to an end, any talk of keeping or not keeping the precepts also ceases. However, only bodhisattvas beyond the seventh and eighth spiritual levels have achieved this freedom of mind and do not have to pay additional attention to the precepts. For the benefit of others they are able to behave as ordinary sentient beings. It is also valid for them to say that they are Buddhas. But it would be a great mistake for people like ourselves to perform actions and make statements that are not in accordance with our actual capacities. For an ordinary sentient being to proclaim that he is a Buddha and to pretend to act like one would be like a beggar claiming to be the president of a country. Would anyone ever acknowledge him as such?

The practice of patience is one of the means to awaken to your true nature. It assists in the cultivation of wholesome deeds and enables you to accumulate the merit necessary for the attainment of Buddhahood and the saving of all sentient beings.

The beginning of spiritual training is similar to patiently trying to tame an ox. An ox that runs wildly around must be lassoed and grazed until it is subdued. Likewise, having embarked on the path of *hwadu* meditation, we must begin by patiently enduring many difficulties. Only by continuing to practice assiduously in this way will we finally awaken. Hence patience, which is the forbearance of what is difficult and unpleasant, is precisely the way to awaken to our true nature. Since it is easy to indulge in unvirtuous actions but difficult to commit ourselves to what is virtuous, the forbearance of what is difficult is also an important aspect of cultivating wholesome deeds. Furthermore, only after awakening to the mind are we truly able to guide others. Thus, the realization of Buddhahood and the saving of all sentient beings is likewise indirectly accomplished through the merit produced by patience.

In addition, the perfection of patience includes refraining from quarreling, not deceiving our own conscience, and not making distinctions. In this way, patience is instrumental in overcoming ignorance. We need to establish our will as firmly as a great mountain. A great mountain is immovable. Likewise, our will should never waver, no matter what hardships we encounter. The ocean embraces and accepts all things within it. Similarly, our minds should be able to accept all circumstances with boundless forbearance.

Often, when suffering from hunger and cold, the determination to practice meditation arises. But when we have a full belly and are warmly clothed, only laziness develops. Since even animals can enjoy such things as a full stomach and bodily warmth, these things can hardly be considered the greatest happinesses of human life. It is only when men and women are engaged in the complete fulfillment of their human obligations that they can experience true happiness.

You should not allow yourselves to be lazy in the practices of giving, morality, and patience. Whatever is noble and worthy, you should perform it diligently and exert a great effort to bring it to completion. But you should not make a show of your virtues. Instead you should perform them secretly, unknown to others.

In Confucianism it is said, "Cultivate virtue in the manner of a thief." This means that you should be as inconspicuous in your actions as though you were secretly trying to steal something. To act secretively here means that you should not be concerned whether others see you doing something or not. Simply go ahead with your action and do it as a matter of course. Those who act virtuously only when others are looking, but do the opposite when others are absent, are mere hypocrites.

There was once a man who spent his time trying to scoop all the water out of the ocean in order to find a lost jewel. Everyday for many years he would go to the seashore and diligently start scooping out the water. One day the god of the ocean asked him what he was doing. He replied that he intended to empty the ocean of water in order to find his lost jewel. Derisively, the god of the ocean told him that since the ocean was forty thousand miles in circumference, he would never succeed in his task. The man then explained to him that even though the ocean may be so vast, it was still finite. And even if he could not empty it in this life, since his future lives were endless he could continue scooping out the water in his subsequent rebirths until the task was accomplished. In the end he was bound to find his jewel. The god of the ocean reflected on this and concluded that this naive person would not only succeed in retrieving the jewel but would also destroy the ocean, thus leaving him homeless. To prevent the latter from happening, he then produced the jewel himself and gave it to the man.

The man in the story was in fact the Buddha during one of his previous lives as a bodhisattva. The search for the jewel is an allegory of the search for the mind. This legend illustrates the kind of effort we need to exert in our practice of meditation. If we combine such determination and innocent simplicity, we can be assured of succeeding in our quest.

Whenever the mind is at ease, peacefulness results. However, true peacefulness is only found upon awakening to the mind. We cannot consider the highest values of mankind to be embodied in material things. The highest value of man can only be realized through awakening to the mind. Thus, we should devote ourselves to the search for spiritual peace by awakening to the ultimate truth that underlies all phenomena.

It is impossible to fill a broken and unclean vessel with pure water. But when water comes to settle in an unbroken and clean vessel, the moon is able to reflect clearly in it. Similarly, the quieter and purer the mind becomes, the more manifest will be the brightness of the wisdom originating from the true nature. Finally, when conceit and all other stains are removed, we will awaken to the immovable mind.

Once mastery over our destiny within birth and death is obtained, we will be finally content. We will understand our role in the world and will no longer be subject to the unsettling influence of the eight winds. To have mastery over our destiny within birth and death means that always and everywhere our minds are at peace. And no longer being prone to the vicissitudes of birth and death, we realize eternal life. Understanding our role in the world means to recognize the attainment of Buddhahood as our goal and set out to accomplish it. Since there is no higher goal than enlightenment, only then will we know true contentment. Gain, loss; fame, disrepute; praise, criticism; pleasure and displeasure—these are the eight winds that give rise to the unsettling waves of discontent in this world.

The doors of our senses should be shut as firmly as the gates of a fortress. Consciousness is continually entering and leaving through these six doors. Therefore, those who are cultivating the mind must firmly secure their consciousness within the gates of the fortress. In this way the six thieves (the sense objects) will be unable to distract us. Only in this manner will we be able to discover peace of mind.

*W*isdom is not a particular thing that can somehow be acquired.

*It is simply that which knows how to eat when we are hungry,
how to sleep when we are tired, and how to use a fan when we
are hot.*

Wisdom is that which makes a vessel into a teacup when it
is filled with tea, a sauce dish when it is filled with sauce,
a rice bowl when it is filled with rice, and a medicine pot
when it is filled with medicine. There is no set method in
the functioning of this wisdom. It is simply that which
knows how to utilize things according to the case at hand.

Do you know what constitutes the brightness of the
mind? Have you ever witnessed the radiance that emerges
from it? An enlightened person is able to directly see this
radiance of the mind. But even if you are unable to actually
see it, you are nevertheless using it right here and now.
This brightness that radiates from the mind is precisely
that which is able to see forms and hear sounds. If it were
absent, we would be unable to either see or hear.

With wisdom we should judge carefully between what
is wholesome and unwholesome in our lives. We should
try and act so that the mind always remains pure, bright,
and unobstructed. We should behave with a sense of firm
conviction in the rightness of what we are doing. To ex-
ercise this kind of wisdom is to wield the sword that dispels
the three poisons of attachment, anger, and ignorance. It is
the perfection of wisdom itself.

*In addition to the six perfections mentioned above we should put
into practice the "four guiding dharmas" as a means of rendering
service to others through all our wholesome actions. In general,
this involves praising the virtuous deeds of others, developing
great compassion, and helping those in difficulty and misery.*

The first of the four guiding dharmas is giving. This entails
not only providing material assistance but also spiritual

help to those in need. In addition to benefiting others, such giving will, according to the karmic law of cause and effect, also bear fruit in our receiving of aid when we are in need ourselves.

The second guiding dharma is loving speech. This means that we should try to guide others with kind and gentle words. Loving speech is to practice loving kindness and compassion in everything we say.

The third guiding dharma is beneficial action. This includes helping others in whatever ways we can through our physical and mental actions. Although beneficial actions may only appear to be of direct aid to others, they are actually the prelude to benefits that will return to ourselves.

The fourth guiding dharma is cooperation. This means guiding others while working together with them. It entails taking into full consideration the character of the other, even to the extent of temporarily adapting one's own behavior in order to inspire trust in the other person.

The ancient masters used to say, "The weight of a single grain of rice offered with devotion exceeds that of Mount Sumeru."

If we are unable to realize the Way now while living in this monastery, eating the rice and wearing the clothes offered to us, then in the next life we will be forced to wear the skin of an ox and to grow horns in order to pay off the debts we have incurred. There are some monks who seem unconcerned about the belongings of the monastery and thus misuse them. But through such misuse they are only creating a debt for themselves. No one else will be able to pay it off for them. The ancients compared such monks to "people who completely wear away their own whetstone while sharpening the knives of others."

Such people may believe that they are causing others to acquire a great amount of merit. But to demand that lay people, as well as those other monks who are supplying the provisions and services of the temple, should make some merit through giving them what they wish or replacing what they have misused is only a way of incurring further debt for themselves. You should remember that there is nothing, not even the tip of a hair, that can be had for free. Everything that you receive from others puts you in their debt. And it is then your personal responsibility to repay it.

Therefore, in order to lighten the burden of your debt, you should use the offerings you receive sparingly. Such frugality will be for your own good. In this regard the ancients said, "If you cannot awaken during this lifetime, you will be unable to digest even a drop of water in the next."

The food you eat, the clothes you wear, and even the electricity you use are all offered to you. The very ground you walk on is provided by a benefactor. Even to drink a single drop of water is to receive alms from those who have offered the land. Your body too is not really yours. It has been given to you through the kindness of your parents. Thus, to live as a monk is to live entirely through the alms donated to you by your benefactors.

A bird that constantly flies here and there runs the great risk of eventually being caught in a net. An animal that roams freely is always subject to the fear of being struck by an arrow.

If you intend to resolve the great affair of birth and death and become a man of the Way, you must be as fearful and cautious as though you were walking on thin ice. During the twenty-four hours of the day, in all the four postures, you must raise a firm resolution as unmovable as a mountain. Your mind must be as tranquil and expansive as the ocean. Accept your hardships with magnanimity; practice diligently with renunciation—then finally you will awaken.

When you have to walk somewhere on a dark night, it is very difficult to clearly see the path ahead of you. You do not know whether the way will consist of mountains, deep gullies, swamps, thorny forests, or rock-covered ground.

One by one you may have to encounter and traverse each of these difficult terrains. But if you do not stop and continue walking carefully throughout the night, eventually the dim light of dawn will appear in the east and gradually become brighter. As the sun rises, the path ahead will become clearer and clearer and the difficult passages will become easier to traverse. It is similar when practicing meditation. Whatever difficulties you face at the beginning, you should learn to endure them all. Whether you are beset by wandering thoughts, overcome with drowsiness, or aggravated by pains in your legs or back, you should never allow them to distract you from the meditation. If you continuously persevere, then suddenly your firm hold on the *hwadu* will appear before you as a wide and boundless path. Being able to see the path distinctly, you should make the firm resolve to swiftly advance. Now, while keeping a firm hold on the *hwadu*, you can confidently allow the mind to be as it is. In due time your original nature will shine forth as brilliantly as the rising sun.

While contemplating the *hwadu* you should be as earnest as someone trying to extinguish a fire burning on his head; as a thirsty man in search of water; as an infant thinking of his mother's breast; as an old man worrying about his lineage dying out; or as a cat intent on catching a mouse.

How great is our feeling of despair when we cannot find a secure refuge and stand at a crossroads completely lost and disoriented?

If we knew that an abundant treasure house were nearby, wouldn't we cast off the suffering of inner poverty and go there? How can anyone enjoy remaining on the dangerous paths within the vast desert of Samsara? Bitter hardship and extreme misery are not innate qualities of man. So let us throw them aside immediately!

Everyone has a native homeland. Have you reached it yet?

If not, then this world will appear to you as a road which never ends. How could you ever delight in such a world? If you wish to reach your homeland, your will must be so firm that you would dare to pull out the eyebrows of a tiger; and your spirit must be so steadfast that you would risk grabbing the beard of a flying dragon. Only then will you reach it.

In the garden of Songgwang Sa there is a dead juniper tree. It was planted there about eight hundred years ago by the Korean National Master Pojo. In front of it there is an inscription which reads: "If I live, you live; If I die, you die."

This has been interpreted to mean that if Master Pojo were to return to life, then this dead juniper tree would also return to life. However, this is not what it means at all. It really means that as soon as you realize your true nature and thereby transcend birth and death, simultaneously do all things in the universe transcend birth and death. Likewise, as long as you remain in delusion, subject and object appear to be separate. But as soon as you awaken, you transcend the duality of subject and object and thereby become a liberated sage.

There are times when wandering thoughts arise and disappear incessantly, the hwadu *is confused with dullness and distractedness, and the force of the defilements seems stronger than ever. At such times of difficulty, you might wonder how you will ever make any progress in your practice.*

Throughout beginningless aeons we have been afflicted by such hindrances. Yet one way to overcome them is to cultivate the following three disabilities: blindness (although you have eyes, not knowing how to see), deafness (although you have ears, not knowing how to hear), dumbness (although you have a tongue, not knowing how to speak).

To be blind, deaf, and dumb in this manner means that whatever circumstances you encounter, whether good or bad, you remain just like a tree or a stone. In this way, by keeping your thoughts plain and simple, your mind will remain unhindered. Even when confronting a thousand or ten thousand different conditions, you should be as still as cold ashes or a withered tree. In this manner no obstacles will bar your way. In the midst of all circumstances try and be like cold water. In this way you will not be subjected to emotional reactions.

If, under all circumstances, you can remain uninvolved, the *hwadu* raised in the morning will stay with you throughout the evening until the following morning. Even though ten thousand years pass by, it will continue unbroken and unshakable. In this way you become a person who has lost his usefulness. For such a person back and front, before and after, disappear. Thus, having no thoughts of going back or moving forward, the *hwadu* remains clear and unmixed. At this time, even though you do not raise the *hwadu*, it will arise of its own accord. And even if you do not intentionally inquire, the questioning will be there.

When an ordinary person begins to practice meditation he may feel that there is something to be cultivated and something to be realized.

But should he experience a great awakening, he would then understand that there is really nothing to be cultivated and nothing to be realized. This is so because there is nothing that can affect the true nature. The accomplished sage is not endowed with more of it and the ordinary person is not endowed with less of it. The difference only lies in the fact that the sage has awakened to his true nature, whereas the ordinary person remains ignorant of it.

Look! The Buddhas and the patriarchs of the ten directions are standing on the tip of this mountain monk's staff.

They are building large monasteries and turning the great wheel of Dharma. With different voices they all proclaim that each sentient being is originally endowed with the wisdom and marks of the Tathagata. If you are endowed with the Dharma eye, say something! What is this?

In the Avatamsaka Sutra *it is stated, "He who wishes to comprehend the state of Buddhahood should purify his mind until it becomes like empty space."*

What does it mean to "purify the mind until it becomes like empty space?" It means to reach a point where it is no longer stained by defilements. The mind is similar to empty space. Depending on the changing conditions, space may be filled with clouds, wind may blow through it, rain and snow may fall through it, the sun or moon may shine within it, or it may be enveloped in darkness. However, none of these things actually affect the nature of space itself. During a rainstorm, it does not get wet. Neither clouds, wind, moonlight, nor darkness affect the way it is. It can never be impeded or obstructed by anything.

The mind truly resembles empty space when it is emptied of all delusive thinking. At this time all thoughts of good or bad, right or wrong, this or that, disappear from the mind. Even the notions of Pure Lands or Samsara, Buddhas or sentient beings, completely vanish. But what must be done in order for all such concepts to disappear?

First you must search for the mind through meditation. By exerting much effort, the root of questioning will become firmly established in the mind. When this questioning is very stable, then, in one moment, everything will dissolve and vanish. At this time, you will realize that the universe that you previously imagined to exist, in fact does not.

Although I could tell you that the universe does not really exist, it would be very hard for you to believe this. While seeming to exist, it does not actually exist. Only when you awaken will you realize this to be the case. It is not something that you can understand through words and letters. For this is the secret of the Buddhas and the patriarchs: "Even though the universe seems real, in fact it is not."

When practicing meditation there are times when it goes well and times when it goes badly. Sometimes it is as smooth as pushing a boat over ice. But you should not then give rise to thoughts of joy. In that way you would be captured by the mara of joy.

At other times it is as difficult as trying to pull an ox into a well. But then there is no need to give rise to thoughts of sadness or failure. For in that way you would become a prisoner of the *mara* of sadness and failure.

At other times you may suffer from headaches, dimness

of vision, or a feeling as though your teeth were falling out. Sometimes when you are walking, it might seem as though on a calm day the wind is blowing or that the earth is shaking when in fact it is not. At such times do not succumb to feelings of fear or anxiety. Do not lose your hold on the *hwadu*. Such things are only temporary states of mind produced by tensions in the body. You will never achieve anything if, at these times, you cease to meditate on the *hwadu*.

Sometimes the body's vital energy rises to the head and creates tension. When this happens, you should hold your will as firm as a mountain and make your mind as calm as the sea. Sit erect on your cushion and gently focus the sense of questioning into a point three fingers below the naval.[15] In this way the *hwadu* will be able to quickly ripen. Eventually the body will come to feel like empty space. It will seem to both exist and not exist at the same time. When mind and body become very light and comfortable, then you will gradually be able to enter the higher states of meditation.

If you wish to awaken to the true nature, you should not search for it outside of yourselves.

Why is this? Because if you seek the true nature outside, you will only succeed in distancing yourself from it. You would be like someone who intended to go eastwards but ended up going to the west. In this regard an ancient master said, "If you throw a clod of earth at a lion, the lion will attack you. But if you throw it at a dog, the dog will chase after it."

Those who have not awakened to the mind live enslaved to circumstance.

They dream not only while they are asleep; even when their eyes are open they live in a dream. This is truly a pitiful situation. Everything we do while remaining ignorant of our true nature is similar to the actions of a blind man who wanders aimlessly from east to west, from the past into the present. Every time we take a step forward or move our hands, our action is unwholesome. Every time we give rise to a thought, our thinking is defiled.

There are people nowadays who think that sentient beings in these degenerate times are unable to make progress through meditation. They believe that it is impossible to perceive one's original nature and realize Buddhahood.

Therefore, they maintain that one should simply recite the Buddha's name or study sutras with the hope to be reborn in a Pure Land. However, this is a foolish practice, because instead of seeking the Buddha within themselves, they continuously look for him elsewhere. But if they were to search for their own mind and awaken to it, they would realize that they themselves are intrinsically Buddhas. Upon awakening to the mind, they will immediately come to be endowed with the observance of the precepts, an understanding of the sutras, and the presence of a Pure Land. When one awakens, this world becomes a Pure Land. There is no Pure Land anywhere else. Therefore, the most effective and true practice is to awaken to the mind.

The nature of the entire universe is your own mind. All things are created by the mind and arise from it. So where is the creator of the universe? Your own mind alone is the creator.

There is no one else who created it for you; therefore, this universe is your own universe. This is true whether you are awakened or not. The universe can be affirmed or negated only because we are here now. If we were not present, there would be no one to make such affirmations or denials. Since we create the universe, how can one then say that we came from anywhere or will depart to somewhere else? In reality, there can never be any such coming or going. Hence, it is meaningless to talk of "going" to a Pure Land. For how can a Pure Land exist elsewhere when in fact it is latent within one's own mind? It is thus a great mistake to ignore the mind and instead just recite the name of Amitabha Buddha with the belief that this will lead you to a distant world created through the forty-eight vows of that Buddha.

There is a well-known saying which declares, "It is difficult for one who is clever and learned in worldly wisdom to encounter the Buddha dharma."

This is a problem for many people who are practicing Zen nowadays. Such persons try to come to an understanding through conceptual thinking alone. They insist that reality accord to the way they think it should exist. However, such worldly wisdom only screens the truth. Through scheming and speculating, it just gives rise to mere cleverness. Without being able to free yourself from such intellectual thinking, it will be extremely hard to encounter the true Buddha dharma. For this reason, those who only practice intellectual Zen are unable to make any progress. Even when sitting in meditation, they are still burdened with all their concepts. They project all of their clever ideas in front of them and only succeed in obstructing themselves. You must reject all concepts at once! Only then can you smoothly enter into and progress with your practice. Just as clouds in the sky obscure the brightness of the sun, so do conceptions prevent the bright light of your original nature from shining forth.

The more deluded your minds are, the more difficult will be your practice. Thus it is all the more important to find a wise teacher to guide you. One of the principal reasons for relying on such a teacher is in order to overcome pride.

Pride is self-destructive because it causes you to imagine that you understand something when in fact you do not. Hence you never ask the advice of others and just let things stay as they are. In addition, to help one heed the words of wise teachers, you need to cultivate an attitude of respect. Not only should you respect your teachers but you need to respect yourselves. This is achieved through seeking a true way of life for yourselves. However, if you consider the life you are leading at present to be sufficient in itself and refuse to acknowledge any other alternative, you will only give rise to further pride.

There are no doors or gates which open to the great Way. You can neither enter it nor leave it. Throughout the Dharma worlds as numerous as the sands along the river Ganges, there is not a single thing which is not permeated by it. It is also called the "secret store of the Tathagata."

There is no movement within the highest truth. It neither decreases nor increases. Throughout the worlds of the ten directions every single phenomenon is completely permeated by all phenomena. Hence, this truth is also called the "ocean of wisdom."

The radiance of the subtle principle, with which all beings are endowed, is extremely brilliant. Whether raising your hands, moving your feet, putting on clothes, or eating food—in every action, it is clear and distinct.

The subtle functioning knows no limits. Thus, the mountain's being high, the ocean's being vast, the flower's blooming, the bird's singing, and each thing's being long or short—there is nothing that is not the true nature.

Upon awakening to your true self, you are called a Buddha: upon forgetting your true self, you are called a sentient being. Human life is very short. It cannot last for long. Who is to blame if you live to no purpose and die in distress?

The Way is to be found within Samsara itself.

Vimalakirti once said that you should practice in the very midst of birth and death. And when your practice develops and you gain a little insight, then do not speak of a sudden or gradual approach. Remember that you can look at Mount Chogye from the north as well as the south.

The Way is nothing special. Over your head you carry the blue heavens. With your feet you tread the great Earth. When you open your eyes you see the sun. And yet you still tire your legs with long sittings!

The Way (Tao) refers to the fact that truth permeates everything from the great truth of the universe to each and every one of its numerous forms. Thus the non-outflow Way is equivalent to the non-outflow truth, that is, the unchanging and unmovable truth that is never subject to any outflow. This in turn refers to the fact that when delusive thinking ceases, the truth appears, the Way brightens, and the original nature becomes clear. All these terms are words that constitute a single thread.

Although the vivid and quiescent light of the mind may shine brightly, do not, under any pretext, give rise to intellection or hold such opinions as "I know" or "I am enlightened." To cherish such opinions without having either penetrated the hwadu *or awakened to the true nature will imprison you in the "palace of delusion."*

At this time, you must further cultivate the attitude of great courage. Since the subtle stream of defilements has not yet been exhausted, you still need to inquire earnestly into the *hwadu*. And as the flow of delusive thoughts is still present, you must become increasingly ferocious. Like a mouse digging its way into a cow horn, you should continuously and uninterruptedly push forward. Suddenly a meshing will occur, similar to when the upper and lower pieces of a millstone come together in a perfect fit. Then the way of words and speech will be severed. The discursive activities of the mind will cease. Without a doubt the "lacquer barrel" of ignorance will be shattered. Your natural and true face will be revealed. You will be able to seize and defeat the ancient masters. You will no longer be deceived by the tongues of spiritual teachers of this world. In a single glance you will clearly see the Buddhas and the patriarchs. You will immediately understand the eighty-four thousand volumes of the Buddhist canon.

Monasteries and meditation centers are the refineries of man.

They are like furnaces that refine the ordinary person and transform him into an accomplished sage. Because gold is so highly valued in the world, people spare no expense in their search for it. First they mine the ore, then they smelt it in a furnace. Only through this process are they able to finally extract the pure gold from the other constituents.

Likewise, the Buddha nature is innate within each of us. But if we do not undergo the process of cultivating the path, it will be impossible to ever discover our true nature and thus transform ourselves from an ordinary person into an accomplished sage.

When the lion's roar echoes among mountains and rivers, the foxes and spirits lose their courage and flee.

When the dragons cause rain to moisten the earth, sentient beings and insentient things are all benefitted. In perfect unhindered freedom birds soar through the sky—they climb upwards, they descend; they fly east, they fly west. While maintaining the mind of non-action, the outstanding person gives rise to great compassion and sets out to save all beings.

All sentient beings are sailing in a boat that is crossing the ocean.

Man is one with the boat. The ocean is one with the land. Everything you see is in constant activity and motion. But there is one thing alone that is majestic yet totally natural. All things rest within its embrace. You are frequently caught up in bustling crowds. But do you ever perceive this one unmoving thing? By understanding it you reach the realm of freedom.

The four great elements break apart from one another. The eye and its objects of sight drift away from each other. Do you know where they go? Upon discovering their destination you will arrive at the jeweled palace. Do you have any of those jewels in your own home?

When you can kick and overturn the earth, and touch the sun with your hands, only then will you have arrived.

In ancient times the Zen monk Gao Tingjian of Zhangzhou once observed the Master Deshan on the far bank of a river. As a distant greeting he put his hands together, bowed, and said, "Haven't you investigated yourself yet?"

Deshan just waved the fan which he was holding in his hand. Thereupon, Gao Tingjian was suddenly enlightened. He then ran off down the bank of the river without even turning his head to look back.

Another monk, Fa Jianyi, made the following remark on this episode: "How strange! Such virtuous meditators as this eminent one are so very difficult to meet. Old Deshan's cudgel was always in use. It was as though he were sowing stars. His blows certainly produced some good monks."

Now let me add a few words. In the past, Deshan waved his fan. Now I raise my fly whisk. Are these two actions the same or different? If you say they are the same, then clouds are covering the clear sky. And if you say they are different, then wind is passing over the surface of the water. May those endowed with the Dharma eye speak out!

The Buddha is mind and mind is the Buddha.

Outside of mind there is no Buddha and outside of the Buddha there is no mind. So why search for the Buddha apart from mind? The Buddhas of the past have gone and the Buddhas of the future have not yet come. So where will you find the Buddha of the present? Just discover your own mind. Then the true Buddha of the present will appear in the world. At such a time you will walk hand in hand with all the Buddhas of the three times. There will be no place that is not a place of enlightenment, and no time when you cannot enjoy the happiness of Nirvana.

The awakened person is similar to white clouds over green mountains.

He is not fettered by any state. Hence there is no right or wrong in any of his actions. In accordance with karmic conditions he moves along like a blue stream in a deep valley, which flows freely through the curves and straights. He is like an empty boat drifting along propelled through the mere rising and falling of the waves. He is like a white gull on a cliff that eats when hungry and, as the sun sets, searches for reeds in which to rest in perfect freedom. I ask you people of the world: who is engaged in this discrimination?

The eyes of the awakened person, who has realized his eternally unchanging true nature, directly perceive the great truth of the universe.

Such a person transcends the past, the present, and the future. He transcends both time and space. Thus, he is obstructed neither by being nor non-being. This is what is meant by liberation. Just as a mirror reflects whatever is created, he sees all phenomena through his great perfect mirror wisdom. He is free from all defilements and attachment—like rain falling gently on the blue ocean. By remaining within the mind of non-action, he has followed the stream and reached the marvel. Now he is vast, boundless, and unobstructed. Conditioned existence has come to an end for him. Birth and death no longer concern him. He realizes all beings to be Vairocana Buddha and everywhere to be a Pure Land of lotus flowers. There is nothing for him that is not sacred. He can truly be called a person who is beyond all things.

N*either sentient beings nor non-sentient things are ever separate from the true nature.*

Hence, this nature is characterized as simply "thus." And because it can be neither increased nor diminished, the sage has no abundance of it and the ordinary person no deficiency. This true nature permeates the entirety of space. The virtue of beholding it is that the world of external objects is simultaneously purified. As the visual sense base is purified through this vision, the other five senses are simultaneously purified. Likewise, the six sense spheres are purified as well. In this way the entire world becomes a Pure Land.

O*nly one thing remains spiritually alive;*
Its remarkable functions are manifold.
From the very beginning, there has been no
    birth and death;
However, do you really understand this?
Having cast aside the six senses and their objects,
Its essence now appears in all its fullness.
The entire earth, with its mountains and its
    rivers, will be one's own home.

Who can pass through the realms of darkness
Bearing gold and silver?
You can face the Lord of Death
With your good and evil deeds alone.

According to conditions,
Your true nature is returning home.
But how could your bleached bones

Ever reach the Pure Land?
For the sake of Dharma, forget the body
And tread the path of enlightenment!
In the same way as all the Buddhas,
As you reach the other shore
You will find your place of origin.

Since your true nature is always present,
It is truly the Great Way.
Since your spiritually active radiance shines
   everywhere,
It is truly the Lord of the ten thousand things.

(A memorial ceremony poem)

CHAPTER EIGHT

The Ten Oxherding Pictures

Thus Samsara is transcended!
Blue mountains cross the waters
Like a sail before the wind.
Flowers bloom on a white rock:
It is spring outside the universe.

1. GOING OUT IN SEARCH OF THE OX

High mountains, deep waters, and a dense jungle
  of grass—
However much you try, the way to proceed
  remains unclear!
To alleviate this sense of frustration, listen to
  the chirping of cicadas.

This picture illustrates the feelings of someone who is
practicing meditation for the first time. He is compared to
a man in search of an ox who has just come outdoors in
order to find it and then catch it with a rope. All of us who
claim to be cultivating the Way usually have to pass through
the difficult stage described here.

What are the pleasures we find in living in the world?
These are to eat well, to wear good clothes, to have wealth,
a good reputation, and a family, and to be able to sleep at

ease. These are all basic physical concerns. However, what we call "cultivation of the Way" runs counter to these concerns. To live in the ordinary world is like flowing along with the current of a river. But to cultivate the Way is like swimming upstream against the direction of the current. Since beginningless time the body has become accustomed to certain comforts. Now one suddenly decides to cultivate the Way through the practice of meditation.

And what is this like at the beginning? It is similar to finding yourself seated in front of a silver mountain or an iron wall. Thus, you encounter "high mountains, deep waters, and a dense jungle of grass." In the midst of all this, "however much you try, the way to proceed remains unclear." At this point you often wonder if the meditation is actually progressing at all. You start to consider various different ways of improving the practice. You find yourself at a complete loss as to what you should do.

After struggling and exerting themselves in this way for a while some people reach such a point of exhaustion that they consider giving up altogether. Although they have tried to practice, they cannot see any progress at all. But one should definitely not give up at this stage. Others will try "to alleviate this sense of frustration" in turning to another kind of practice. They may start to pray to the Buddha, repeat the Buddha's name, or recite some sutras. In such ways, their sense of frustration is alleviated somewhat. But actually they are just listening "to the chirping of cicadas." This does not mean that they literally go outside and listen to cicadas. It refers to their engaging in all those activities other than the practice of meditation in order to remove their feelings of frustration.

2. SEEING THE FOOTPRINTS

> A tangle of thorny bushes: the faint murmur
> of running water.
> But here and there are footprints—is this the right
> path?
> If you want to pierce its nose and tie it up, do not
> rely on someone else's strength!

Your fundamental task is not that of trying in various ways to make things easier for yourself. If you intend to cultivate the mind, then you have to practice meditation. Yet even though you try, the meditation may not seem to progress. So you must remind yourself of the need to do such practice. In this way you will be able to check and control the distracted thoughts which pull you away from the meditation.

While you are struggling around with much hardship in the "tangle of thorny bushes," you may hear "the faint murmur of running water." This refers to the intrusion of certain external obstacles that occasionally interfere with the practice. The "faint murmur of running water" means that a *mara* is present. It may be that the people around you, your family, or some harmful friends start telling you that you may as well drop the idea of meditation since it doesn't seem to be getting you anywhere. But instead of listening to them you should carefully pay heed to the words of the Buddhas, the patriarchs, and other wise spiritual teachers. In doing this, the determination to persevere in the practice will grow in your mind.

Having made this decision, "if you want to pierce [the ox's] nose and tie it up, do not rely on someone else's strength!" A true and authentic practice entails being able to stand firmly on your own ground without depending on the support of others. You have to make all the effort yourself. You cannot borrow anyone else's strength. The Buddha may have delivered eightly-thousand discourses; the patriarchs may have repeatedly spoken of "pointing to the mind, seeing the nature and becoming a Buddha"; and other teachers may have given all kinds of advice on how to develop one's practice. Nevertheless all their words can only serve as guidelines to indicate the path. Having entered the path, you have to tread it yourself.

There are still people who, instead of making the effort themselves, hope that there are others who will be able to give the strength needed to proceed. They think that simply by depending on a certain teacher their practice is bound to progress. They like to believe that just by visiting a good teacher who will give them a few blows, they will automatically be saved. But this is never the case. Just because your practice makes no progress by itself, there is no reason to expect that somebody else will be able to supply such progress. When there is no progress, it is simply because you are not exerting sufficient effort yourself. To think otherwise is foolish. It is ridiculous to complain that no one is helping you when you yourself are not making any effort. Therefore, "if you want to pierce its nose and tie it up, do not rely on someone else's strength!"

At this point you may also start to notice that "here and there are footprints." This may lead you to believe that now you are surely on "the right path." Your task is to follow these footprints. You have to proceed entirely on the basis of your own effort. Following these footprints is like climbing a high mountain. Even if someone were to stand motionless at the base of such a mountain just staring at it for ten thousand years, this would be of no use at all. Step by step, he must follow the path to the top himself. Of course, the one who walks quickly will get there before the one who walks slowly. But no matter how you proceed, you have to go on your own.

3. SEEING THE OX

Among willow branches swaying in the spring
  breeze an oriole is singing.
How can the sparrow experience his joy in calling
  to his mate?
Isn't the moonlight glimmering in the forest
  my home?

As you persevere in following the tracks of the ox you finally begin to glimpse its tail now and again. In this way you first catch sight of the ox.

For a Korean, the oriole's song seems to say, "prettily, prettily, brush your hair and come over." It is this kind of mating song that I refer to in the verse. Yet "how can a sparrow," who cannot sing in the same way as an oriole, "experience the oriole's joy in calling to his mate?" Or how can a mere sparrow appreciate the wonderful time the golden oriole has in flying back and forth between the trees in pursuit of his mate?

After practicing for some time, one gradually starts to make progress. This is like peering at the distant moon and watching its light glimmering faintly in the forest. Such light is similar to the dim, flickering glow of a firefly. Having persevered in one's meditation, occasionally a little insight will light up for a few moments like the glow of a firefly, die, light up again, and then die again. This is what is referred to by the line, "Isn't the moonlight glimmering in the forest my home?"

What you experience at this stage is something that you have never heard or seen before. Recognizing now that such a thing exists, you reflect that it is probably correct to keep going in this direction. At such a moment the mind has to make an important decision. In striving to maintain the *hwadu,* you have been advancing with great difficulty through a patch of thorny bushes. Now, in the midst of all this, a little moonlight starts to shine in the forest. Although you are encouraged to continue, this is still an uncertain and ambiguous time.

4. CATCHING THE OX

> *Advancing with difficulty; the ox's nose is*
> *pierced.*
> *But this fiery nature is hard to control.*
> *Dragged here and there, you stray through*
> *cloud-covered forests.*

"Advancing with difficulty" means that you have to endure physical hardships without caring whether you live
or die. It is at such a time that "the ox's nose is pierced."
Yet even though its nose is pierced, its "fiery nature is
hard to control." Whatever you do, the ox will always try
to retreat quickly and run away. At times, though, the
practice makes good progress, like that of a boat being
pushed over ice. But after a while it ceases to be so easy and
becomes as difficult as trying to force a horse to drink water
when it doesn't want to. No matter how close you succeed
in bringing the horse to water, it will keep avoiding it and
running off. To control immediately the "fiery nature" of
the ox is indeed difficult.

"Dragged here and there, you stray through cloud-
covered forests." In such a place the moon only shines
sporadically. After you have caught the ox and with a great
effort pulled it toward you for a while, it will suddenly

pull you off in another direction. You try to pull it back, but again it manages to drag you elsewhere. It goes on and on like this. Now you are struggling with great difficulty in a cloud-covered forest. The clouds are dense and the forest is thick. And you keep on straying here and there, catching hold of the ox and trying to pull it in your direction.

What exactly is this difficult time? It refers to the stage when the meditation is composed partly of the *hwadu*, partly of distracted thoughts, and partly of sinking into dullness. At this time, these three factors seem to be competing with one another: at some times you find yourself in a state of dullness, at other times beset with distracting thoughts, and at other times concentrating on the *hwadu*. This is a very difficult period because now you are really fighting with the ox.

5. HERDING THE OX

Fearing that it may fall into a steep and perilous path,
You hold it tight with whip and bridle,
* and with the strength of both legs firmly hold*
* your ground.*
Once past this critical moment, the ox comes
* following you.*

It is at this stage that you learn to handle the ox in the right way. "Fearing that it may fall into a steep and perilous path" refers to the reaching of a certain stage in the practice when you are again beset with the doubt that no progress is being made. You reflect that in spite of your

effort and enduring of hardship, the meditation is proceeding neither quickly nor well enough. Once more you are tempted to give up and instead study some sutras or recite some mantras. You might even contemplate becoming the abbot of a rich monastery or marrying a pretty girl and settling down to a worldly existence.

No matter how much effort you seem to be putting into the practice, it does not ripen as swiftly as you would wish it to. Soon all kinds of thoughts start to trouble your mind. You wonder: By practicing in this way am I really getting anywhere? What am I doing? Now a *mara* has entered your mind. You become aware of the danger that the ox "may fall into a steep and perilous path." This can be a very frightening time. So you have to "hold it tight with whip and bridle, and with the strength of both legs firmly hold your ground." Otherwise it may actually break loose and stumble into the perilous path.

If you exert a great deal of effort for a while, then you will pass the "critical moment." Thereafter, "the ox comes following you." This is so because once you cross over that difficult point you will have succeeded in finally taming the ox somewhat. Then you will realize that even if you went back to the world it would be of no use. However well you feed and clothe the body, however comfortable and secure you can make it, at one moment it will become nothing but a heap of ashes. Although beforehand you were tempted by such things, now you decide to relinquish them. You also decide to renounce all worldly positions, wealth, and fame; the prestige you could have in the religious order by being an abbot; and the respect you would receive from lecturing on the Dharma should you study the sutras. You now become determined to realize your own mind and become an accomplished being through the practice of meditation alone.

Once such a firm resolve has arisen in the mind, then you truly seize the abode of the *hwadu*. Now that the ox is being tamed in this way, the *hwadu* is firmly held and does not move. For such a person when he goes, it is practice; when he comes, it is practice. Having passed over the critical moment, the ox now obediently follows without your having to grab hold of it and pull it.

6. RIDING THE OX BACK HOME

Sitting astride the ox, the noble person happily returns.
The sound of his flute mingles with the crimson sky:
he has discovered the garden of joy.

Who else could know about this endlessly pleasurable taste?

Once you have passed the critical moment and the practice has become somewhat more leisurely, then what is called "the single homogenous mass" begins to emerge.

Now when you sit, the *hwadu* is simply there just as it is. Although you sit all day, you are unaware of sitting; although you walk all day, you are unaware of walking; although you eat all day, you are unaware of eating; even if you sleep all day and night, you will be unaware of having slept. Such is the state of the single homogenous mass. When going, the *hwadu* is going; when coming, the *hwadu* is coming; when eating, the *hwadu* is eating; when talking, the *hwadu* is talking; when sleeping, the *hwadu* is sleeping; even when defecating, it is the *hwadu* that is defecating. The *hwadu* is no longer constantly appearing and disappearing. When coming or going, it is just as it is.

When a person at this state sits, he is like a great unmoving mountain. When sitting, he just sits. He truly has the bearing of a mountain. Thus "sitting astride the ox, the noble person happily returns."

While riding the ox, you play the flute. You are now not at all concerned even if you go into a patch of mist or a field of thorns. The meditation has reached the point where you can practice even in the middle of a busy marketplace. You can meditate while gathering wood in the mountains, while weeding the vegetable fields, or while working in the rice paddy.

What does it mean to say that "the sound of his flute mingles with the crimson sky" and that "he has discovered the garden of joy"? When playing the flute while astride the ox, the person can now handle the ox in a leisurely fashion. Left to himself, the ox will just follow the way it has to go. Now that it has been tamed, however much you ignore it, it will no longer go anywhere that is not allowed. As for yourself, no matter whether you are sleeping or moving around, standing or lying down, no one else will be aware of the inner composure you have attained. At this sixth stage the practice really begins to develop with every step.

7. FORGETTING THE OX, THE MAN RESTS ALONE

Bright moon and cool wind: what a splendid home!
Sitting all alone, the ox has gone away.
Even if you doze until sunrise, what use would
*   be a whip and bridle?*

The bright moon is rising and a cool wind is blowing: this is truly the best house of all. What a splendid home it is!

Now the ox is gone. First you had to make an effort to hold on to the ox; then, after some time, it began to follow you of its own accord. At this stage you do not have to pay it any attention at all. It proceeds correctly by along the way by itself.

"Even if you doze until sunrise, . . ." This means that after sitting all night, unaware of the passing of time, while you are dozing with your back slightly bent, you quietly look up and cannot tell whether it is still nighttime or whether day has broken.

Many years ago in Haein Sa monastery, Kyongho Sunim would just sit quietly all day and night with his back slightly bent. Upon observing this, the sutra lecturer who lived below wrote him a note which said: "Since the venerable old monk is always dozing with his head down, it would seem that he has nothing better to do than to sleep." In reply, Kyongho Sunim answered: "Since there is nothing left for me to do, my only task now is to sleep." Because the ox is just as it should be, there is no need to whip it any more. Therefore, at this stage, even if you only doze, your practice will still keep advancing.

Kyongho Sunim then added: "Sitting on the high seat, there is no need to think of this or that. One sits in *samadhi* without any thoughts at all." Such a person remains in *samadhi* irrespective of whether he is sitting or dozing. He continued: "Sitting without any thoughts, one abides in tranquillity and suchness. Thus one advances in one's natural state. So why do you disturb me by stirring up a little breeze? Instead of letting me sleep quietly in the forest, why do you make me float in the air?" At this stage you proceed entirely by yourself and need neither whip nor bridle.

8. THE OX AND THE MAN ARE BOTH FORGOTTEN

> *Since even space has collapsed, how can*
> *obstacles remain?*
> *Could a snowflake survive inside a burning*
> *flame?*
> *You cheerfully come and go: how could you not*
> *always laugh?*

Both the ox and the man have now been forgotten, and you are sitting in silence and emptiness. At such a time "even space has collapsed." In our present state, all phenomena—

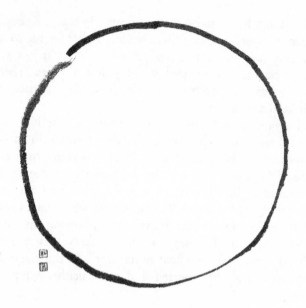

including space—are experienced as existing. But at this time, space collapses. This is finally the moment of awakening. In order for the original nature to appear, it is necessary for even space to collapse.

"Could a snowflake survive inside a burning flame?" In the midst of such a state, the Buddhas and the patriarchs are of no use any more. For this is the time of "striking down the Buddha and striking down the patriarchs." Since the Buddhas and patriarchs are both of no use, how can you distinguish between ordinary and accomplished beings? Who would be ordinary? And who would be accomplished? Not even a single snowflake could survive here: the Buddhas and patriarchs are of no use to you now.

"You cheerfully come and go: how could you not always laugh?" It is fine to come and fine to go. It is fine to lie on your back and fine to lie on your belly. You may go as you please through the three unfortunate realms. Whether you are in hell, among the hungry ghosts, or amid the animals, everything is fine. If you find yourself in hell, in heaven, or in the Buddha lands, you can only laugh.

9. RETURNING TO THE ORIGINAL PLACE

> *My very own treasure is recovered: all those efforts*
>   *spent in vain!*
> *It would be better to have been blind, deaf,*
>   *and dumb.*
> *The mountains and water are just as they are!*
>   *So is the bird among the flowers.*

Finally you realize that you have recovered your very own treasure, which you had forgotten all about. When you quietly reflect on it, you recognize that all of the exertions you put into the practice were actually unnecessary. Now when you simply open your mouth, this is a teaching of Dharma; when you walk along, this is also a teaching of Dharma. Such a person is just like this: there is nothing else to it. There is nothing that is not Dharma. In fact, it would have been better had you been blind, deaf, and dumb. Why? Because then you would not have been dragged into doing so many useless tasks. Now "the mountains and water are just as they are." Such is the Dharma teaching of inanimate things.

10. APPEARING IN THE MARKETPLACE TO TEACH AND TRANSFORM

Ragged and starving you approach the market and the streets.
Even covered in dust, why would the laughter cease?
The bees and butterflies are happy because flowers have bloomed on a withered tree.

In order to be of benefit to sentient beings, you are free to act in whatever way you see fit. You cultivate the way of the bodhisattva in wandering here and there through the streets and marketplaces. You perform the deeds of a bodhisattva: if someone asks you for whatever you are wearing or eating, you simply give it to him. Whatever you do, it is fine. If circumstances are favorable, you smile; and if cir-

cumstances are unfavourable, you still smile. With a laugh you take things as they are—like a fool! At this time, flowers have bloomed on a withered tree. Thus, whatever such a person does, he is pleasing to all sentient beings.

This concludes my explanation of the oxherding pictures. I am afraid I have not done this very well and have just succeeded in giving rise to numerous distracted thoughts. As the ancients said:

When a bird flies, its feathers drop;
When a fish stirs, the water is muddied.

Notes

1. For the general historical background of Buddhism in Korea
   I have drawn upon Park Chong-hong, "Buddhist Influence
   on Korean Thought," *Korea Journal,* Korean National Com-
   mission for Unesco, Vol. 4, no. 5, pp. 4–7; Kwon Sang-no,
   "History of Korean Buddhism," *Korea Journal,* Vol. 4, no. 5
   pp. 8–14; Moon Sang-hee, "A Historical Survey of Korean
   Religion," *Korea Journal,* Vol. 14, no. 5, pp. 14–24; Kil Hui-
   song, "State and Sangha in Korean History," *Korea Journal,*
   Vol. 21, no. 8, pp. 41–48; and Sørensen, H. H., "The Unique
   Position of Korean Buddhism and its Influence on the De-
   velopment of Buddhism in the Far East" (unpublished paper).
   On the introduction of Zen into Korea, Sim Chae-Ryong,
   "Son Buddhist Tradition in Korea: as Represented by Chinul's
   Pojo Son," *Korea Journal,* Vol. 26, no. 8, pp. 14–31; Suk Do-
   Ryun, "Sun Buddhism in Korea II" *Korea Journal,* Vol. 4,
   no. 3, pp. 41–47; Robert Buswell, *The Korean Approach to
   Zen: The Collected Works of Chinul* (University Press of
   Hawaii, 1983) pp. 9–14.
   For the history of Buddhism in modern Korea, Seo Kyong-
   Bo, "Characteristics of Korean Zen," *Korea Journal,* Vol. 12,
   no. 5, pp. 29–37; Pak Kyong-hun, "Buddhism in Modern
   Korea," *Korea Journal,* Vol. 21, no. 8, pp. 32–40; Wi Jo-kang,
   "The Secularisation of Korean Buddhism under Japanese
   Colonialism," *Korea Journal,* Vol. 19, no. 7, pp. 42–47.

On the history of Buddhism in China, Kenneth K. S. Ch'en, *Buddhism in China: A Historical Survey* (Princeton University Press, 1964); Arthur F. Wright, *Buddhism in Chinese History* (Stanford University Press, 1959).

For the life of Wonhyo, Cho Myung-ki, "Prominent Buddhist Leaders and their Doctrines," *Korea Journal,* Vol. 4, no. 5, pp. 15–21; Rhi Ki-yong, "Wonhyo and his Thought," *Korea Journal,* Vol. 11, no. 1, pp. 4–9; Ko Ik-chin, "Wonhyo and the Foundations of Korean Buddhism," *Korea Journal,* Vol. 21, no. 8, pp. 4–13.

On the life of Uich'on, Cho Myung-ki (*op. cit.*); Buswell, (*op. cit.*), pp. 14–17.

For the life of Chinul, Buswell, (*op. cit.*), pp. 17–71; Pak Song-Bae, "The Life of the Ven. Chinul," *Korea Journal,* Vol. 11, no. 2, pp. 19–23.

On the life of T'aego, Seo Kyong-bo, *A Study of Korean Zen Buddhism Approached through the Chodangjip* (Ph.D. dissertation, Temple University, 1960; mimeographed reprint, Seoul, 1973) pp. 321–29.

For the life of Sosan, Cho Myung-ki (*op. cit*); U Chong-sang, "High Priest Hyujong," *Korea Journal,* Vol. 13, no. 2, pp. 22–27; Seo Kyong-bo (*op. cit.*), pp. 336–50.

On the life of Kyongho, Suk Do-ryun, "Modern Sun Buddhism in Korea II," *Korea Journal,* Vol. 5, no. 2, pp. 27–32; Seo Kyong-bo (*op. cit.*), pp. 357–71.

2. Buswell (*op. cit*), p. 27.
3. For a full account of this episode, see pp. 121–26.
4. Buswell (*op. cit.*), p. 67.
5. Buswell (*op. cit*), p. 66.
6. For a translation of the verses and comments of Gaoan Shi-yuan (Kao-an Shih-yuan), see D. T. Suzuki, *A Manual of Zen Buddhism* (Grove Press, 1960), pp. 129–34.
7. In Korea, a stone lion is still found nowadays by the roadside at the entrance of most towns and cities. Master Kusan also used the name Stone Lion as a pen name for his works of calligraphy.
8. The origin of the *hwadu* "What is this?" or "What is it?" is traced to the encounter between Nanyue Huairang (677–744) and the Sixth Patriarch, Huineng: "Asked by the patri-

arch where he came from, he (Huairang) replied, 'From the monastery of Master Hui An at Song Shan.' The patriarch asked, 'What thing is it and how does it come?' The master was speechless, and eight years later one day he suddenly experienced some spiritual awakening and said to the patriarch, 'I have experienced some awakening.' The patriarch asked, 'What is it?' The master replied, 'To say it is like something misses the mark.' The patriarch asked, 'Can it still be practiced and experienced?' The master replied, 'Although its cultivation and experiencing are not uncalled for, it cannot be sullied.' The patriarch said, 'Just that which cannot be sullied is protected and thought of by all the Buddhas. It is so for you and also for me.' " (Quoted from Lu K'uan Yü, *The Transmission of the Mind Outside the Teaching* (Rider, 1974), p. 33).

9. This section was adapted in part from: Master Kusan, recorded by Bhiksu Ham Wol, "The Path of the Hua-T'ou: Practical Instructions to Western Students of Ch'an," first published in the *International Buddhist Forum Quarterly* (Autumn/Winter 1978–79).

10. For the origin of the *hwadu* "No!" see p. 69. "The cypress in the courtyard" is an answer Zhaozhou once gave to the question, "Why did Bodhidharma come from the West?"

11. *See* p. 121.

12. A state of nervous tension caused by a disorder in the rising of the body's vital energy (C. *qi*; J. *ki*; Skt. *prāṇa*).

13. It is customary in Korea that when a lay-supporter of the monastery dies, his relatives may also request, in addition to the usual prayers and ceremonies for the deceased, a Dharma lecture to be given on his behalf or specially dedicated to him.

14. The first seven sections given here treat the topic of the six perfections. The remaining sections are not arranged according to any specific themes.

15. The solar plexus area (K., *tanjon*; C., *tantian*).

Glossary

Accomplished Being. One who has experienced awakening.

Amitabha Buddha. The Buddha responsible for the creation of the Western Pure Land through the force of his forty-eight vows to save sentient beings.

Aśvaghoṣa. A renowned Indian Buddhist master who was probably active around the first century A.D. He is somewhat doubtfully attributed with the authorship of the *Awakening of Faith in the Mahāyāna,* a scripture widely studied in China and the other Buddhist countries of East Asia.

Ānanda. The cousin and personal attendant of the historical Buddha, Śākyamuni.

Avalokiteśvara. A bodhisattva who personifies compassion and is widely worshiped in all Mahāyāna Buddhist countries.

Avataṃsaka Sutra. The *Hua Yen* (Flower Garland) scripture of Mahāyāna Buddhism. *See* pp. 10, 20.

Avīci. According to Buddhist cosmology, the deepest of the eight hot hells, where beings are subjected to uninterrupted torments.

Awakening. The realization of one's true nature through meditation.

Barrier of the patriarchs. The final obstacle to awakening to be broken through by means of meditation.

Bhikṣu. A fully ordained Buddhist monk.

Bodhidharma. The Indian meditation master who brought Zen from India to China in around A.D. 520.

Bodhisattva. A being who aspires to attain enlightenment in order to save others.

Bodhi tree. A pipal tree in Bodh Gaya, India, under which Śākyamuni Buddha sat for seven days before realizing full enlightenment.

Buddha. See p. 55.

Buddha nature. See pp. 54–55.

Buddha realm. (1) A non-samsaric Pure Land created through the power of a Buddha's enlightenment; (2) the world as it appears to one who has realized enlightenment.

Buddha world. See Buddha realm.

Chogye, Mount. The mountain on which Songgwang Sa monastery is situated. It is named after Mount Caoqi (Ts'ao-ch'i) in China, the site of the monastery of Huineng.

Common being. An ordinary being who has not yet experienced awakening.

Concentration (Skt. samādhi). One-pointed absorption of mind developed through meditation.

Dahui (Ta-hui: 1089–1163). One of the first Chinese Zen masters to advocate the use of the hwadu.

Defilement. The negative conceptual and emotional obscurations of the mind.

Deshan (Te-shan: 780–865). A Chinese Zen master noted for his rough style of teaching.

Dharma. A Sanskrit term meaning either the teaching of Buddhism; principle or law; or phenomena in general.

Dharma body. See Dharmakāya.

Dharmadhātu. The universe in its totality; the underlying principle of reality.

Dharma-ending age. The period in which Buddhism undergoes decline.

Dharma eye. The state of mind that directly perceives the ultimate truth.

Dharmakāya. The dharma body; the spiritual principle of Buddhahood.

Diamond Sutra (Skt. *Vajracchedikā prajñāpāramitā-sūtra*). A Mahāyāna text of the Perfection of Wisdom category that expounds the view of emptiness.

Eight deeds of the Buddha. The eight major phases of the historical Buddha's life.

Eight winds. Gain, loss; fame, disrepute; praise, criticism; and pleasure, displeasure.

Eighty-four thousand. A traditional expression meaning "very many."

Emptiness. In the Indian Mādhyamaka philosophy, the ultimate nature of phenomena; here, often used to describe either non-existence or the absence of all mental and physical sensation experienced at some stages of meditation.

Five aggregates. The basic constituents of conditioned existence: materiality, feelings, discernments, volitional factors, and consciousness.

Forty-ninth-day ceremony. A memorial ceremony performed on behalf of the deceased on what is believed by some Buddhists to be the final day in the intermediate state between death and rebirth.

Four positions. Lying down, sitting, standing, and walking.

Ganges. The most sacred river in India.

Great Mirror Wisdom. That aspect of the enlightened mind that reflects all phenomena equally.

"Hak!" The abrupt shout used by Korean Zen masters to shock their disciples into a sudden awareness of their true nature.

Huineng (638–713). The sixth patriarch of Chinese Zen.

Hwadu. See p. 53–54.

Hyobong Sŭnim. The teacher of Kusan Sŭnim. *See* pp. 42–43.

Indra. One of the principal celestial divinities of Indian cosmology, regarded as a tutelary deity in Buddhism.

Koan. *See* discussion of *hwadu*, pp. 53–54.

Li. A Chinese measure of distance, approximately half a kilometer.

Linji (Lin-chi; J. Rinzai: d. 867). A major Chinese Zen master.

Lion's roar. The utterances of the Buddha, who, among ordinary men, is comparable to a lion among animals.

Lion's throne. The seat of the Buddha.

Lord of Death. Yama, the traditional Indian personification of death.

Mahāyāna. Literally, the "great vehicle." A name for the teachings of the Buddha that deal with the bodhisattva's path to enlightenment.

Maitreya. The forthcoming Buddha; regarded as the next enlightened world teacher to appear on earth.

Mañjuśrī. A bodhisattva who is depicted as the personification of wisdom.

Mantra. A mystical formula usually composed of Sanskrit syllables. It is often associated with a particular Buddha or bodhisattva and is recited in a continuous and repetitive manner.

Māra. Negative or demonic influence; often depicted in a personified form as the demon Mara.

Mind. *See* pp. 54–55.

Nanquan (Nan-ch'uan: 748–834). A well-known Chinese Zen master, a disciple of Mazu and the teacher of Zhaozhou.

Nirmāṇakāya. The "transformation body" of the Buddha, that is, the physical form he manifests in the world.

Nirvana. The quiescent state realized through the cessation of suffering and defilement.

Non-doing (C. *wuwei*). Originally a Taoist term; used to translate the Buddhist concept of the "unconditioned"; here, it is used to refer to the non-attached actions of an enlightened being.

One mind. *See* p. 54.

Original face. *See* p. 54.

Patriarch. A realized being through whom the lineage of understanding has been passed down from the Buddha to the present generation.

Pojo. The posthumous name of the Korean master Chinul, the founder of Songgwang Sa. *See* pp. 17–22.

Pure Land. A non-samsaric realm created by a Buddha. Here, it is often used to denote a heavenly realm in general.

Pure Land Buddhism. A school of Buddhism that emphasizes devotion to the Buddha Amitabha and the repetition of his name as the most effective means to salvation.

Questioning. *See* p. 38.

Quiescence and vividness. A balanced state of meditation in which the *hwadu* appears brightly and one's senses remain tranquil and controlled.

Samādhi. See Concentration.

Samantabhadra. A bodhisattva often regarded as the personification of great action.

Sambhogakāya. Literally, the "enjoyment body" of the Buddha; here, it is understood as the "fruition body," that is, the fruit of a Buddha's past actions as a bodhisattva.

Samsara (Skt. *saṃsāra*). The illusory cycle of repeated birth and death.

Sarira. Small mineral-like droplets of varying sizes and colors that are sometimes found among the cremated remains of monks and other religious practitioners. In Buddhist countries, they are considered to be an indication of spiritual maturity and are frequently enshrined and worshiped as sacred relics.

Śākyamuni. The historical Buddha, who lived in India about five hundred years before Christ.

Six perfections. The six virtues to be cultivated by a bodhisattva: generosity, morality, patience, effort, meditation, and wisdom.

Six realms. The six regions of samsaric existence: the abodes of the celestials, titans, humans, animals, hungry ghosts, and denizens of hell.

Six thieves. The six sense objects (forms, sounds, smells, tastes, textures, and ideas) that "steal" the attention.

Sŏktu Sŭnim (1882–1954). The teacher of Hyobong Sŭnim.

Spiritual advisor. One who is capable of guiding others along the path to awakening.

Spiritual level. Ten stages of advanced bodhisattva practice outlined in the Mahāyāna scriptures.

Śrāmaṇera. A novice Buddhist monk.

Stepping off the hundred-foot pole. An analogy often used in Zen to describe one of the final stages in meditation before an awakening is reached.

Sŭnim. The Korean title of address for monks and nuns.

Sutra (Skt. *sūtra*). A discourse given by a Buddha.

Tang (T'ang) dynasty. The Chinese dynasty that ruled from 618 to 907.

Tathāgata. Literally, "one who has gone thus"; a traditional epithet for a Buddha.

Ten directions. The eight points of the compass, the zenith, and the nadir.

Three times. Past, present, and future.

Three worlds. The planes of desire, form, and no form.

True nature. *See* p. 54.

Vairocana. The name of a Buddha; according to the Avataṃsaka Sutra, the Buddha whose body is said to symbolically constitute the universe; he can also represent the *dharmakāya*.

Vimalakīrti. A wise layman at the time of the Buddha whose teachings are recorded in the *Vimalakīrti-nirdeśa-sūtra*.

Vinaya. The body of ethical rules and disciplines for Buddhist monks and laypersons prescribed by the Buddha.

Way (C. Dao [Tao]). A classical Chinese concept best known through its use in Taoism, but also appropriated by the Buddhists to translate the Sanskrit term *mārga* (path). Here it is used to refer both to the universal principle of one mind, or Buddha nature, as well as to the particular path of practice that brings one more and more into harmony with the one mind.

Yakṣa. A terrifying spirit.

Yogācāra. An idealist school of Mahāyāna Buddhist philosophy. Also known by the names Vijñānavāda and Cittamātra.

Zhaozhou (Chao-chou: 778–897). A famous Chinese Zen master of the Tang dynasty from whose dialogues many koans were formulated.

Zongjing (Tsung-ching: 904–75). Better known as Yongming (Yungming); a noted Chinese Zen master.

Made in the USA
Las Vegas, NV
14 April 2024

88691512R00114